The Copper Bay Cookbook

THE·COPPER·BAY
COOKBOOK

Recipes from the Queen Charlotte Islands

MARIA ERNST

HARBOUR PUBLISHING

Published by
HARBOUR PUBLISHING
P.O. Box 219
Madeira Park, BC Canada V0N 2H0

Cover and interior graphic design by Gaye Hammond
Printed and bound in Canada

Canadian Cataloguing in Publication Data

Ernst, Maria.
  The Copper Bay cookbook

Includes index.
ISBN 1-55017-064-3

  1. Cookery — British Columbia — Queen
Charlotte Islands.   2. Cookery, Canadian — British
Columbia style.   I. Title.
TX715.6.E75 1992   641.59711'12   C92-091163-3

*To my husband, Walter, and
our daughters, Andrea and
Barbara, who never gave up on
my first feeble attempts, but
with love, kindness, and faith
made a passable cook out of me.*

*With love to the memory of my
mother and grandmother, two
courageous women who
planted the seeds.*

My thanks go to Amanda Brown, who not only typed the manuscript so beautifully, but corrected patiently the many mistakes and put up with my handwriting. To Mabel (Binky) Stevens for her "courier service." To Diane King for her valuable advice and encouragement.

Thank you, all.

Contents

Preface

Putting this cookbook together was not only enjoyable, it became a journey though my life, evoking many memories of family and friends.

I was born in Thuringia, a part of the former East Germany, and grew up surrounded by a doting family in a rambling, comfortable old house. I can still see my grandmother's kitchen, with the large stove where her cook moved the many pots back and forth to find the correct place with the right temperature. What aromas — tantalizing, exotic, and comforting.

During the war, while my father was away, we took our Sunday noon meal (Mittagessen) with our grandparents. And Omi always turned the gathering into a festive occasion. How hard my grandmother and her cook must have worked to produce such delectable meals, as we all had to cope with food rations and many ingredients were not available. We were fortunate enough, though, to be able to grow all our own fruit and vegetables, and my great-grandfather's farm provided us with the rest. Substituting and improvising became an art. Mother tried to follow her grand-mother's motto: Meals must not only be delicious, they also have to be good for you.

When we moved to West Germany, and later to Canada, so many changes were taking place that I did not receive the instruction my grandmother and mother had had as young women. Then I trained as a nurse and became so absorbed in my profession that there was no time to learn how to cook, and no need. When I met my husband Walter, only his kindness made our marriage survive. I could not even boil an egg! Our little daughters learned that when Daddy was home, we had tasty meals, while with Mother, alone, we just got by.

My husband Walter loves the outdoors and has a keen interest in fishing and hunting, and in 1970 we decided to leave Victoria and move to the Queen Charlotte Islands to build and operate the Copper Bay hunting and fishing lodge. Walter holds the Guide–Outfitter's licence for Graham Island, a large part of the Haida Gwaii. Somebody had to do the cooking — me!

Mother came, advised and helped. We studied cook-books; my sister-in-law, Marianne (an excellent cook), arrived from Austria; many friends offered endless suggestions. After some trials and tribulations, heavy tummies, and kind shakings of heads when offered second helpings, I finally had some successes. Then I started to enjoy cooking, trying out my own recipes and incorporating old with new. Guests began to come back and ask for special dishes. I was on my way!

At first, the lodge was just a small log building. Our two daughters, Andrea and Barbara, didn't go to board-ing school until they were sixteen, so we have many memories of juggling guests, family members, dogs and cats in that tiny space. We enlarged the lodge in 1979, and now we are able to accommodate seven or eight guests at a time.

We are open all year round, and our guests come from all over the world. Many people stay with us for the fishing and hunting, but we also have visitors who come to rest, walk the beaches and enjoy the solitude and peace of these beautiful islands.

I do all the cooking and run the place myself most of the time, except during very busy months, when Andrea and Barbara come from Victoria to give us a hand. Our two eldest grandchildren, Natasha and Séàn, are already very capable and willing as well. All of our children and grandchildren have very strong ties with the Copper Bay Lodge, having grown up with the lodge – the business we run and the special place we call home.

Because of our wild and wonderful location, there are times when it is impossible to have all the necessary cooking supplies on hand. I have lots of experience experimenting and improvising! Walter and our guests keep the kitchen well stocked with game and fish, and many of the recipes in this book were invented when I substituted these fresh local foods for meat in my traditional family recipes. The results have been excellent.

Even more creative improvising is sometimes required. For instance, these islands are quite often battered by strong storms. On a few occasions, we have been left without electricity for two or three days – that's several meals! The wood fires keep the lodge cozy and the water boiling, but some storms have helped me create new dishes. One evening, I had made a casserole and planned to cook a red cabbage as the accompanying vegetable. The casserole warmed beautifully on the "Fisher," and I ended up inventing Our Own Rotkraut Salat (see p. 79). We served by candlelight, and my improvised dish turned out to be a favourite at the lodge.

When I was growing up, my grandmother and mother gathered home-grown products for the table as often as possible, so I was introduced to organic gardening at an early age. With those memories and my nursing background, with its emphasis on health and nutrition, I found it quite natural to plan menus with mostly whole foods and organic products. The recipes in this book contain almost no refined or over-processed foods, yet they are inexpensive and simple to prepare.

I hope you will enjoy my collection of recipes as much as I enjoyed creating them. Follow them exactly for good results, but don't be afraid to use your imagination. You will find, as I did, that with very little effort and cost, you can create meals that taste good, look beautiful, and nourish the people you love.

A Few Kitchen Hints

Your cookware can make all the difference in the results of your efforts in the kitchen. I use Lifetime cookware, and there are several other good products designed for gentle, even heat distribution.

For an extra-specially rich gravy, add a tablespoon of dry sherry before serving.

Store cottage cheese upside down. It keeps longer.

If you thaw fish in milk, the frozen taste will be replaced by a "freshly caught" flavour.

Save cooled water from boiled eggs and give the drink to your house plants. The minerals will do wonders.

Add a tang to whipped cream or custard by adding a tablespoon of sweet sherry.

Brown sugar dissolved in a teaspoon of canned milk and brushed over a pie crust makes a lovely glaze.

To cut very fresh bread, hold the knife under hot water for a few minutes before slicing.

To reheat bread or rolls, place them in a paper bag. Preheat oven to 400°F. Sprinkle the bag with water, turn off the preheated oven (with the oven off there is no danger of the bag catching fire) and leave the bag in the oven for 10 minutes.

Always read a recipe from start to finish *before* you start preparing it.

Converting Measurements

WHEN YOU KNOW:	YOU CAN FIND:	IF YOU MULTIPLY BY:
ounces	grams	28
pounds	kilograms	0.45
ounces	millilitres	30
pints	litres	0.47
quarts	litres	0.95
gallons	litres	3.8
Farenheit°	Celsius°	5/9 or .56 (after subtracting 32)

WEIGHTS & MEASURES

3 tsp	1 tbsp	15 mL
4 tbsp	¼ cup	60 mL
5 ⅓ tbsp	⅓ cup	79 mL
8 tbsp	½ cup	118 mL
16 tbsp	1 cup	237 mL
1 fluid oz	2 tbsp	30 mL
8 fluid oz	1 cup	237 mL
16 fluid oz	4 cups/1 quart	473 mL

EQUIVALENTS

1 cup butter/margarine	237 mL = ½ lb	227 g
1 cup cheese, grated	237 mL = ¼ lb	114 g
1 cup eggs	237 mL = 4–5 whole eggs *or* 8 egg whites *or* 12 egg yolks	
1 cup flour	237 mL = ¼ lb	114 g
1 envelope gelatin	15 mL = ¼ oz/1 tbsp	7 g
1 cup lard or shortening	237 mL = ½ lb	227 g
juice of 1 medium lemon	45 mL = 1½ fluid oz/3 tbsp	21 g
1 cup chopped nuts	237 mL = ¼ lb	114 g

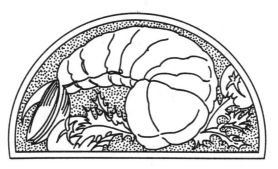

Appetizers

Hot Anchovy Canapés

Serves 5.

2 2-oz. cans flat anchovy fillets
2 medium cloves garlic, minced
1 tsp tomato paste
1½ tbsp. olive oil
2 tsp lemon juice *or* cider vinegar
freshly ground black pepper to taste
8–10 slices fresh French bread (each ¾" thick)
1 tsp finely chopped fresh parsley

Drain the anchovies of all their oil and soak them for 10 minutes in cold water. Pat them dry thoroughly with paper towels. Place them in a heavy bowl with the garlic and tomato paste. Mash with a wooden spoon until the mixture is a very smooth purée, or put into blender and blend on high speed for 5 seconds. Slowly dribble in the oil, stirring constantly until the mixture is the consistency of mayonnaise. Stir in the lemon juice and a few grindings of pepper.

Preheat oven to 500°F. Under the broiler, brown the bread slightly on one side. While the bread is warm, spread the anchovy mixture on the untoasted side and press into bread with the back of a fork. Reduce oven temperature to 350°F. Arrange the bread on a baking sheet and bake 10 minutes. Sprinkle with parsley and serve at once.

Hot Tuna Canapés

Mix flaked tuna with Our Favourite Mayonnaise to taste (see p. 86). Add halved stuffed olives. Season with Worcestershire sauce. Spread on toast strips and sprinkle with grated cheese. Place under broiler until cheese melts. Serves 4–6.

Avocado Canapés

Mash pulp of one ripe avocado. Season with ¼ tsp sea salt, ⅛ tsp paprika, and 1 tsp lemon juice. Spread on toast strips and sprinkle imitation bacon bits on top. Bake at 350°F just until heated through. Serves 4–6.

Potted Cheese

Makes 1½ cups.

>   2 cups grated cheddar cheese
>   ½ cup unsalted butter, softened
>   2 tsp crushed coriander seeds
>   ½ tsp crushed cumin seeds
>   freshly ground black pepper to taste

Beat all ingredients together until soft and fluffy, or purée in blender for a minute or so. Use as a spread for crackers or fingers of toast, or as a sandwich spread. Store remaining Potted Cheese in the refrigerator, tightly wrapped.

Smoked Salmon or Steelhead Toasties

Place paper-thin slices of smoked fish on thin slices of buttered whole wheat toast. Garnish with a little homemade cucumber pickle.

Cheese Shrimp

Spread cream cheese on small whole wheat crackers. Lay medium-sized shrimp on top and press down gently. In the centre of each curled shrimp, place a stuffed olive. Chill before serving.

Vienna Slices

Very low in calories! Makes 30–40 slices.

    1 cup cottage cheese
    4 tsp minced onion
    ¼ tsp seasoned salt
    5 large, thin slices of white or brown bread
        (homemade is best)
    10 small Vienna sausages

Mix cheese, onion and seasoned salt well. Trim crust from the bread slices. With a rolling pin, roll out bread; spread cheese mixture on slices. Place 2 Vienna sausages on each slice, end-to-end, and roll tightly (jelly-roll fashion). Wrap in waxed paper and refrigerate. At serving time, cut each roll into 6–8 crosswise slices.

Mushroom Hors d'Oeuvres

A delicious concoction very easily prepared ahead of time, this appetizer is wonderful served around a fire before a dinner party. Makes 18.

6 tbsp unsalted butter, softened
9 slices white bread
9 slices brown bread
3 tbsp finely chopped shallots
½ lb mushrooms, finely chopped
2 tbsp whole wheat *or* unbleached white flour
1 cup whipping cream
½ tsp sea salt
⅛ tsp cayenne
1 tsp lemon juice
1 tbsp chopped fresh parsley
2 tbsp chopped chives
3 tbsp Parmesan cheese

Preheat oven to 400°F. Butter 18 small muffin cups with 2 tbsp of the soft butter. With the mouth of a drinking glass, cut the bread slices into 3″ discs. Press bread into the muffin tins. Bake 10 minutes.

To prepare filling, melt the remaining 4 tbsp butter in a deep skillet. Add the shallots and cook a few minutes until transparent. Add mushrooms. Cook and stir several minutes until any extra moisture has evaporated. Remove from heat and thoroughly mix in flour. Stir in cream, bring to a boil, and simmer until thickened. Add salt, cayenne, lemon juice, parsley and chives. Correct to taste, and cool.

Reduce oven temperature to 350°F. Fill the bread-forms with the mushroom mixture and top with grated Parmesan. Bake 10 minutes.

Cucumber Sandwiches

These delicate morsels can be served as appetizers or at tea. Serves 6.

1 cucumber, peeled and very thinly sliced
10 slices buttered bread, crusts removed, sliced
    thin (homemeade is best)
freshly ground black pepper to taste
sea salt to taste

Place the cucumber slices on 5 slices of the bread. Sprinkle with a little pepper and salt. Cover with remaining slices of bread and cut each sandwich into 4 triangles. Arrange on a serving plate.

Shrimp Spread

Serves 4–6.

1 can shrimp *or* 1 cup fresh shrimp (reserve juice
    if can is used)
1 tbsp light cream (if fresh shrimp is used)
8 oz cream cheese, softened
2 tbsp chives
¼ cup chopped black olives
¼ cup chopped celery
lemon juice to taste

Add shrimp juice or cream to cream cheese. Blend until smooth in mixer or by hand. Add remaining ingredients. Serve on small pieces of toast as an appetizer, or use as a sandwich filling.

Walnut Spread

Here is a delicious, quick, vitamin-rich sandwich filling, wonderful on toast, crackers or fresh pumpernickel bread. Serves 4–6.

> 1 cup walnuts, ground in blender or food
>   processor
> pinch of sea salt
> mayonnaise (Our Favourite Mayonnaise, p. 86, is
>   ideal)

Combine the nuts and salt, and add just enough mayonnaise to moisten.

Cheese Walnut Spread

Children love this one, so make it often — it's good and good for them! Serves 4–6.

> 1 cup walnuts, ground in blender or food
>   processor
> ½ cup soft cream cheese
> French dressing

Combine the walnuts and cream cheese, and add just enough French dressing to moisten.

Asparagus Cups

We first tasted this dish while on vacation in Scotland. It is delicious for brunch on a Sunday morning. Serves 6.

8 slices brown bread, crusts removed
½ cup butter, melted
8 oz fresh asparagus
6 eggs, beaten
½ cup whipping cream
freshly grated black pepper to taste
1 tsp sea salt

Preheat oven to 400°F. Lightly flatten bread with a rolling pin. Press the bread into a Yorkshire Pudding tin and brush with half the melted butter. Bake 10 minutes until crisp and brown.

Trim ½" off the bottom of the asparagus and tie spears in two bundles. Put 2" salted water into a small, deep pan. Stand the asparagus upright in the pan. Cover with a domed lid of foil so the asparagus is cooked in the steam. Cook 15–20 minutes until just tender, then drain well.

Meanwhile, put the eggs, cream, seasoning and remaining butter in a pan and cook, stirring, until the eggs are done. Cut the tips of the asparagus and reserve. Chop the remaining asparagus and stir into the egg mixture. Divide among the cups and garnish with the asparagus tips.

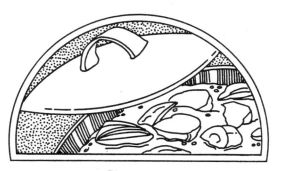

Soups

Lentil Soup

Simple but very delicious and nutritious is our lentil soup. You may substitute table salt for the dulse salt, but dulse salt provides iodine, potassium, calcium, iron, zinc and magnesium, as well as traces of essential vitamins. Serves 4–6.

2 cups lentils (organically grown is best)
1 large onion, sliced
2 large carrots, chopped
1 tbsp honey
2 whole cloves
3 whole cloves garlic
½ tsp basil
½ tsp thyme
3 tbsp unsalted butter
1 tsp dulse salt
½ tsp freshly grated black pepper

Rinse the lentils well. Combine all ingredients, cover with water and simmer until tender, 1–1½ hours. Check occasionally, and if liquid has evaporated, add boiling water as needed.

Split Pea Soup

Here is another old favourite, from my mother's kitchen. Serves 4–6.

    2 cups green split peas
    6 cups cold water
    2 medium onions, finely chopped
    4 large stalks celery (including tops), finely
        chopped
    2 medium potatoes, chopped
    4 cups milk (fresh or canned)
    2 tsp sea salt, or to taste
    2 tsp Spike (available in health food stores)
    freshly ground black pepper to taste
    2 cloves garlic, crushed
    Croutons (see p. 39)
    ½ cup imitation bacon bits

Soak the split peas overnight if desired. Soak in the 6 cups cold water, in a 4-quart pot.

Cook together the peas, onion, celery and potatoes until all are tender, about 1 hour if the peas were soaked; 2 hours if not. Put the soup through a strainer or use an egg beater to blend it. Add milk and seasonings. Serve with croutons and imitation bacon bits.

Variations:

1. Omit potatoes. Make a white sauce of 4 tbsp unbleached flour, 4 tbsp butter and 4 cups milk (see p. 38). Stir white sauce into soup.

2. Serve with wieners, sliced thin and added just before serving.

Peanut Soup

The fun in this unusual soup lies both in the prep-
aration and the flavour. Children love it, and the
soup provides the protein of peanut butter and the
nourishment of chicken soup. I got the recipe from
a wonderful lady who helped me with my children
when they were small, and was aware of my early
struggles in the kitchen. I lost this treasured recipe
for a while, but fortunately found it just in time for
the grandchildren. Serves 4. The recipe can be dou-
bled.

> 3 cups chicken bouillon *or* stock
> ⅓ cup peanut butter
> 1 small onion, finely chopped
> 1 clove garlic, minced
> 1 stalk celery, finely chopped
> ½ bay leaf
> ½ tsp hot red pepper flakes
> ½ tsp soy sauce
> Croutons (see p. 39)

Gradually whisk the bouillon into the peanut butter.
Add remaining ingredients and bring to a boil. Simmer, stirring occasionally, until the vegetables are
soft, about 45 minutes. Remove bay leaf before serving the soup in mugs. Sprinkle croutons on top.

Rice Soup

Serves 4.

6 cups beef or chicken stock
⅔ cup brown rice
1 tsp sea salt
2 eggs
3 tbsp fresh lemon juice

Bring the stock to a boil. Add the rice, cover and cook gently until the rice is tender, about 60 minutes. Add salt. Beat the eggs and lemon juice in a bowl. Gradually add about ½ cup of the stock to the bowl, stirring constantly. Return the egg-lemon mixture to the soup pot. Heat over very low heat, stirring constantly. Take care that the soup does not boil. Serve at once.

Bean Soup

Serves 4.

1 cup white beans
1 bay leaf
1 tsp thyme
1 onion, chopped
1 carrot, chopped
1 potato, peeled and cubed
1½ tbsp olive oil
freshly ground black pepper to taste
sea salt to taste
1½ tbsp unsalted butter
1½ tbsp unbleached flour
pinch brown sugar
1–2 cloves garlic
Croutons (see p. 39)

Soak beans overnight.

Cook beans with bay leaf, thyme, onion, carrot, potato, olive oil, pepper and salt until beans are soft.

Melt butter in a skillet. Add flour, cook and stir constantly for 1–2 minutes. Add 3–4 tbsp of soup liquid to skillet. Mix until smooth and starting to boil. Add to soup; slowly bring to a boil again. Remove bay leaf, add brown sugar, crush garlic onto top and serve with croutons.

Stilton Soup

A very British soup! T. C. Litler-Jones, who has been fishing with Walter for many years, always brings us a wheel of Blue Stilton on his annual visit. Caldwell's stay is always a delight, as he is quite an accomplished cook who has given me many useful suggestions. The following recipe is one of his favourites. Serves 4.

4 tbsp unsalted butter
1 onion, finely chopped
2 stalks celery, chopped
3 tbsp unbleached flour
3 cups chicken stock
3 tbsp dry white wine
½ cup crumbled Blue Stilton cheese
¼ cup grated Rat Trap cheese *or* extra-old white
    cheddar cheese
1 cup milk
¼ cup whipping cream
freshly ground black pepper to taste
sea salt to taste
Croutons (see p. 39)

In a saucepan, melt the butter over low heat. Sauté the onions and celery 5–7 minutes. Stir in the flour and cook for 1 minute. Remove from heat, stir in chicken stock and wine, return to the stove and bring to a boil. Simmer 30 minutes. While stirring, add cheese, milk, cream, pepper and salt. Put soup through strainer and reheat, but do not boil. Sprinkle croutons on top.

Kartoffel Suppe (Potato Soup)

Potato soup is an institution in Germany. In my parents' household, it was served on a "crisis day" when everybody did something that had not been planned, and the time for cooking had become limited. Served with frankfurters, the soup is a complete meal. Serves 4–6.

6 large potatoes, peeled and cubed
3 carrots, scraped and diced
2 onions, chopped
2 leeks *or* 4 stalks celery, sliced
4 sprigs fresh parsley, stem and all
2½ tbsp unsalted butter
7–8 cups meat or vegetable stock
freshly ground black pepper to taste
sea salt to taste
½ cup whipping cream *or* yogurt
Croutons (see p. 39)
chopped olives

In a large pot, combine all ingredients *except* cream, croutons and olives, and cook until vegetables are tender, about 40–50 minutes. Stir in cream, and watch that the soup does not come to a boil. Serve with croutons and chopped olives.

At home, we browned diced bacon and sprinkled it on the soup before serving. As I use bacon only when absolutely necessary, I substitute 2–3 tbsp imitation bacon bits.

Cream of Cauliflower Soup

Serves 4.

2 cups cold water
2 cups chicken stock
1 cauliflower (about 1½ lbs)
4 tbsp unsalted butter
⅓ cup unbleached flour
1 cup milk
¼ tsp white pepper
1 tsp sea salt
⅛ tsp ground nutmeg
1 egg yolk
¼ tsp lemon juice

Bring water and stock to a boil in a 3-quart saucepan. Separate cauliflower into florets, drop into boiling liquid and boil 8–10 minutes (the florets should be tender, but still firm). Remove the cauliflower and set aside.

In a 4-quart saucepan, melt the butter over medium heat. Reduce heat to low, stir in the flour and cook 2 minutes, stirring constantly. Watch that the flour does not get too brown. Stirring constantly with a whisk, pour in the stock and the milk, and cook until the mixture comes to a boil, is smooth and starts to thicken. Simmer 2 minutes. Add the cauliflower, pepper, salt and nutmeg. Simmer, partially covered, 10–15 minutes longer.

In a separate bowl, beat the egg yolk. Add ¼ cup of hot soup to the bowl, a tablespoon at a time. Return the egg mixture to the soup and heat for a further 2 minutes, stirring a few times. Do not let the soup boil. Add lemon juice.

Should you wish a smoother, creamier soup, put vegetables and stock through a sieve before you add the egg concoction.

Onion Soup

This recipe is inspired by the best onion soup I ever tasted. It was made by my Great Aunt (Tante) Gretel. Serves 4–6.

2½ cups thinly sliced onions
¾ cup water
4 tbsp unsalted butter
1 tbsp unbleached flour
6 cups stock
1 tsp Maggi or Worcestershire sauce
sea salt to taste
freshly ground black pepper to taste
paprika to taste
Croutons (see p. 39)

Cook the onion in the water until the water is absorbed. Melt the butter and sauté onion until light brown. Remove from heat. Stir in flour until the onions are coated. Pour in 1 cup of the stock and, while scraping sides and bottom of pan, bring just to the boiling point.

In a large saucepan, pour the remaining 5 cups of stock. Mix with the onion-flour mixture and the Maggi. Cover and simmer 1 hour. Add seasonings and serve with croutons.

Tomato Soup

When we children were ill, we would be given tomato or chicken soup, served with dry toast. Their aromas never failed to stimulate our appetites and, therefore, our recovery. Serves 4.

White Sauce:
2 tbsp butter
2 tbsp unbleached flour
2 cups milk
sea salt to taste
white pepper to taste
grated nutmeg to taste (optional)
a few tablespoons whipping cream (optional)

2 cups stewed or canned tomatoes
½ cup water
2 tsp brown sugar
2 whole cloves
1 tbsp chopped onion
½ tsp sea salt
unsalted butter

To make the White Sauce, melt the butter in a heavy saucepan over low heat. Stir in the flour and cook 3–5 minutes. Pour in milk a little at a time, stirring slowly and constantly (I use a whisk) until smooth. Add a bit of salt. Increase the heat and stir constantly until the sauce comes to a boil. Now reduce heat to low and simmer 4 minutes, stirring occasionally to prevent the sauce from sticking. When thickened, add pepper, more salt if you wish, and nutmeg if desired. For a richer sauce, add a few tablespoons of cream.

Variation: For Parsley Sauce, add 2 tbsp finely chopped fresh parsley.

To complete the Tomato Soup, simmer remaining ingredients together for 20 minutes. Put through strainer, stir well and pour into hot white sauce. Dot with butter and serve at once.

Classic Chicken Soup

Serves 4.

4 green onions, sliced
4 cups chicken stock
2 eggs, slightly beaten
1 cup watercress leaves
1 tsp soy sauce *or* Worcestershire sauce (optional)

Cook green onions in stock for 3 minutes. Add eggs and stir until the eggs form threads; add watercress. Add soy sauce or Worcestershire if desired and serve at once.

Croutons

Serve these crunchy, tasty morsels with your favourite soup.

2 slices bread (homemade is best)
4 tbsp butter
½ cup olive oil

Cut bread into cubes. Heat butter and oil in a large skillet. As soon as it is hot, add bread cubes and turn heat to medium-high. Toss cubes so that they brown evenly on all sides. Remove with a slotted spoon and drain on paper towels.

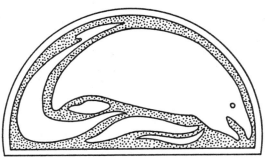

Fish

Lomi Salmon

This recipe comes from a Sandspit lady. It is delicious spread on toast fingers or slices of whole grain or pumpernickel bread. Serves 4–6.

1½ lbs fresh or frozen salmon (thawed)
1½ tbsp coarse pickling salt
juice of 1 lemon
6 medium tomatoes
1 cup finely chopped green onion

Wash salmon and pat dry. Rub with salt and sprinkle lemon juice on all sides. Place in glass bowl. Cover and refrigerate 12–14 hours, turning once or twice (the salt and lemon juice "cook" the salmon). Rinse well in cold water; drain and squeeze, and pat dry with paper towels. Remove bones and skin. Cut salmon into small pieces, then shred with a fork or your fingers. Remove any remaining small bones. Peel tomatoes and chop fine. Add to the salmon with the green onion. Mash together and refrigerate several hours; serve icy cold.

Crab Quiche

During one steelhead season, US President and Mrs. Carter came to stay with us. They were most charming and appreciative guests. Among the entourage of Secret Service men, we had our local RCMP officer as "watchdog" at Copper Bay. One day he found out about a fresh shipment of crabs, which he offered to prepare for me. Unfortunately his method of cooking them was far from perfect, and the result was a large amount of watery and somewhat tasteless crab meat! So I searched desperately to find a recipe that would camouflage the crab, and the following was a great success—so delectable that Mrs. Carter asked for the recipe. Serves 4.

    4 oz Swiss cheese, sliced
    1–9″ unbaked pastry shell
    ½ lb crab meat
    2 green onions, sliced
    3 eggs, beaten
    1 cup light cream
    ½ tsp sea salt
    ¼ tsp dry mustard
    ½ tsp grated lemon rind
    dash ground mace
    ¼ cup slivered almonds

Preheat oven to 325°F. Arrange cheese slices over bottom of pastry shell. Top with crab and green onions. Combine eggs, cream, salt, mustard, lemon rind and mace until well mixed and pour over crab meat. Top with almonds and bake 45 minutes or until set. Remove from oven and let stand before slicing.

Salmon or Steelhead Burgers

Children and adults alike love these burgers! Makes 6.

1 16-oz can salmon *or* 2 cups cooked and flaked salmon
½ cup chopped onion
¼ cup olive oil
⅓ cup salmon liquid *or* milk
⅓ cup + ½ cup dry white bread crumbs (best if made from homemade bread)
2 eggs, beaten
1 tsp dry mustard
¼ cup chopped fresh parsley
½ tsp sea salt
olive oil for frying
1 tbsp sweet pickle
⅓ cup mayonnaise (homemade is best)
6 buttered hamburger buns

Drain fish, reserving the liquid. Flake and remove skin. Cook the onion in the ¼ cup olive oil until tender. Add salmon liquid or milk, ⅓ cup of the bread crumbs, eggs, mustard, parsley, salt and fish. Mix well. Shape into 6 burgers and roll in the remaining ½ cup bread crumbs. Heat more olive oil in a heavy skillet and fry burgers 3–5 minutes. Turn carefully and fry 3–4 minutes longer until brown. Drain on paper towels. Stir pickle into mayonnaise. Put a burger on the bottom of each bun. Top with 1 tbsp or so of the mayonnaise mixture. Top with the other half of the bun and serve.

Salmon or Steelhead Medley

Serves 4.

1 16-oz can salmon *or* 2 cups cooked and flaked
   salmon
¼ cup minced onion
¼ cup unsalted butter, melted
3 tbsp unbleached flour
4 ½ cups liquid (all the liquid from the salmon
   plus enough milk to make 4 ½ cups)
½ tsp sea salt
dash cayenne
¼ tsp freshly ground black pepper
½ cup whipping cream
¼ cup sweet sherry
2 tbsp cognac
1 tbsp finely chopped fresh parsley

If using canned salmon, drain it, remove skin, and
don't forget to keep the liquid. In a saucepan, sauté
onion in butter until transparent. Stir in the flour;
remove from heat. Bring the salmon liquid and milk
to a boil and add to onion mixture. Return to heat,
stirring constantly until sauce is thick and smooth.
Stir in salt, cayenne, pepper, cream, sherry and cognac. Add salmon and parsley. Serve on rice or toast.

Fish Cakes

We eat fish at least three times a week during the season. Some guests insist on having fish dishes every day while they stay with us. As we have some fishermen at Copper Bay for three weeks at a time, it becomes a real challenge to produce a different and tasty meal every day. Thanks to reliable favourites like these fish cakes, we manage quite well. One of our guests, a dear, elderly man from the British Isles who has been coming to stay with us for years and loves his meals, once suggested that a parsley sauce would enhance the cakes tremendously. And it does. This recipe serves 4.

¼ cup butter
1 medium onion, chopped
2 cups cooked *or* canned fish
1 cup soft bread crumbs
2 eggs, slightly beaten
1 tsp sea salt *or* dulse salt
½ tsp freshly ground black pepper
¼ cup whipping cream *or* evaporated milk
whole wheat flour *or* wheat germ
vegetable oil

In a small saucepan, melt the butter and sauté onion until tender. Combine with all other ingredients, *except* whole wheat flour and vegetable oil, in a large bowl. Mix thoroughly. With wet hands, form into patties and roll in flour or wheat germ. Fry slowly in hot vegetable oil until brown on one side. Turn and brown on other side. Serve at once.

Baked Steelhead or Coho

A recipe I have copied over and over again at the request of guests is this baked steelhead trout (superb) or coho salmon. It has always been a great success and it is a very festive meal. Prepare it ahead of time, and you can enjoy your dinner guests while the fish is baking. One warning, though: the fish has to be eaten right after baking—don't let it stand around! Or it can be chilled thoroughly (if any is left) for a most delicious sandwich spread when mixed with mayonnaise. Serves 6.

> 1 whole steelhead trout or coho salmon (4–5 lbs, dressed)
> 1½ tsp sea salt
> ½ cup dried mixed vegetables (available in health food stores)
> 1½ cups chopped onion
> 1 medium bay leaf, crumbled
> 2 cloves garlic, crushed
> ½ cup unsalted butter
> 3 cups soft bread crumbs
> 2 tbsp chopped fresh parsley
> ½ tsp dried rosemary
> dash of freshly ground black pepper
> Sauce Hollandaise (recipe follows)

Rub the inside of the cleaned fish with 1 tsp of the salt. Place fish on a well-greased piece of aluminum foil on a cookie sheet. (Make sure the foil is large enough that you can lift the baked fish to a warmed serving platter when it is done.)

Cook the dried vegetables, onion, bay leaf and garlic in 6 tbsp of the butter until vegetables are tender. Add the bread crumbs, parsley, rosemary, pepper and the remaining ½ tsp salt. Toss lightly.

Preheat the oven to 400°F. Stuff the fish loosely and brush with the remaining butter. Tail and fins must be covered loosely with foil. Bake 45 minutes or until the fish flakes easily with a fork. Serve on a warmed platter with Sauce Hollandaise, brown rice and a tossed salad.

Sauce Hollandaise

Makes about 1 cup.

    4 egg yolks
    3 tbsp hot water
    ½ cup butter
    sea salt to taste
    dash of freshly ground black pepper
    2 tbsp lemon juice

Beat egg yolks and water in double boiler over hot water for 1 minute. Melt butter and pour into egg mixture. Season with salt and pepper and cook, stirring, until thick. Add lemon juice. Serve at once (if you do not serve immediately, do not cover the sauce).

Salmon or Steelhead Quiche

This is an excellent luncheon or dinner dish — not only delicious, but also quick and practical. The quiche can be prepared ahead of time and baked while you chat with your guests. Serve it with a green salad or a cole slaw (see pp. 79, 80) and you have a nutritious, tasty meal. Serves 4–6.

1–10″ unbaked pastry shell
1 large can salmon or steelhead trout (a tall
    Mason jar or equivalent), drained and flaked
1⅓ cups grated Rat Trap cheese *or* extra-old
    white cheddar cheese
¼ cup chopped green onion or chives
1⅓ cups milk
4 eggs
½ tsp sea salt
dash of freshly ground black pepper
3–4 tbsp grated Parmesan cheese

Preheat oven to 350°F. In the bottom of the pastry shell, spread salmon, Rat Trap cheese and onion. Beat milk, eggs, salt and pepper together and pour into shell. Sprinkle the Parmesan cheese on top. Bake 30 minutes, or until a knife inserted off-centre comes out clean. Let stand 10 minutes in the oven with the door ajar before serving.

Salmon or Steelhead Rice Casserole

This is a very popular dish at the lodge. We have one guest who asks for it twice a week. Serves 4–6.

1 large can salmon or steelhead trout (a tall
   Mason jar or equivalent)
2 cups cooked brown rice
2 tbsp butter
1 large onion, chopped
6 tbsp chopped celery
2 cans mushroom soup *or* 2½ cups white sauce
   (see p. 38)
1½–2 cups milk
2½ cups white or whole wheat bread crumbs
   (best if made from homemade bread)

Preheat oven to 350°F. In a large mixing bowl, flake fish. Add cooked rice and liquid from fish. Heat butter and add chopped onion and celery; sauté until tender. Add to salmon, mixing lightly. Place mushroom soup or white sauce in a separate bowl; gradually blend in milk. Place half of the bread crumbs in the bottom of a buttered casserole dish, add alternate layers of fish mixture and sauce. Cover with remaining crumbs. Bake uncovered for about 45 minutes.

Steelhead Grillées

One year, Walter was asked to participate in an International Wildlife Convention in Paris, and friends invited us to stay with them at their home. As Walter had caught a beautiful steelhead before our departure, the fish travelled with us to France, where we presented it to our delightful hostess. The trout was served to us as broiled fish steaks with an herb butter – a most delicious dinner. The recipe works equally well with fresh salmon. Serves 6.

Cut the steelhead trout or salmon into 8 slices (steaks), each 1″ thick. Melt ½ cup unsalted butter. Cut 1 lemon into slices. Preheat the broiler for 10 minutes.

Dry the steaks with paper towels and brush both sides with melted butter. Arrange the steaks on the rack of the broiling pan, and broil 3 minutes on each side, 3–4″ from the heat. Baste with pan drippings or the remaining butter. Sprinkle with sea salt and freshly ground black pepper to taste. Broil for another 3 minutes. Turn the steaks over, baste again, and broil 6–8 minutes longer. Baste once more during the final minutes of broiling. When done, the steaks will be firm when touched. Transfer them to a warmed platter and garnish with lemon slices. Serve with Herb Butter.

Herb Butter

Soften ½ cup unsalted butter and beat until fluffy. Add 2 tbsp chives, 2 tsp minced garlic, 4 tbsp chopped fresh parsley; sea salt and freshly ground black pepper to taste.

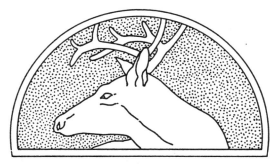

Meat and Game Entrées

Chicken Paprika

*Here is another dish from the kitchens of Austria —
hearty and healthy, and it tastes great. Try to use a
"free range" chicken. Not only are they delicious, but
they certainly are much better for your health. Serves
4–6.*

1 3-lb frying chicken, cut up
sea salt
2–3 tbsp olive oil
1 cup finely chopped onion
½ tsp minced garlic
1½ tbsp sweet Hungarian paprika
1 cup chicken stock
2 tbsp unbleached flour
1–1½ cups sour cream *or* yogurt

Wash the chicken. Pat the pieces dry with paper
towels and salt them generously. In a 10″ skillet, heat
the olive oil over high heat until a light haze forms
over it. Add as many chicken pieces, skin side down,
as will fit in one layer. After 3 minutes, or when the
pieces are golden brown on the bottom, turn them
with tongs and brown the other side. Remove pieces
as they brown and replace them with uncooked ones.
Pour off the fat, leaving only a thin film. Add the onion
and garlic and cook over medium heat for about 10
minutes, or until golden. Remove from heat and stir
in the paprika. Keep stirring until the onions are well
coated. Return the skillet to the heat and add the
chicken stock. Bring to a boil, stirring in the brown
bits from the bottom and sides of the pan.

Return the chicken to the skillet. Bring the liquid
to a boil again, then turn the heat to its lowest point

and cover the pan tightly. Simmer the chicken about 30 minutes, or until the juice from a thigh runs yellow when pierced with a small sharp knife. When the chicken is tender, remove it to a platter. Skim the surface fat from the skillet.

In a mixing bowl, stir the flour into the sour cream or yogurt with a wire whisk, then return it to the skillet. Simmer until the sauce is thick and smooth, about 8 minutes. Return the chicken and any juices to the skillet. Baste with the sauce, simmer 3 minutes to heat through, and serve.

Brown Game Stew

This stew comes out right every time, made with game or beef. Cook dumplings in the stew if you wish (see p. 68), and serve it with a cole slaw (see pp. 79, 80). Serves 4–6.

    1 lb boneless stewing meat
    2 tsp sea salt
    ½ cup whole wheat or unbleached flour
    meat drippings
    2 cups water
    2 potatoes, diced
    1 onion, sliced
    3 carrots, diced
    1 cup green beans, fresh or canned

Cut meat into 1″ cubes, sprinkle with salt, roll in flour and brown in drippings. Add water and simmer 2–3 hours. Add vegetables and continue cooking until vegetables are done, about 30 minutes.

Hunter's Stew

This very Hungarian recipe makes a superb venison stew that is easily prepared ahead of time. It tastes even better when reheated. In Hungary, it is traditionally served with a green salad. Serves 6.

2 cups brown rice
6 cups water
2 tsp sea salt
8 slices bacon, chopped
1½ cups finely chopped onion
1 tsp minced garlic
1 cup scraped and sliced carrots
¼ cup cider vinegar
3 lbs boneless venison or beef chuck, cut into 2" cubes
freshly ground black pepper to taste
2 medium green peppers, seeds and ribs removed, cut into slices ¼" wide and 2" long
1¼ cups beef stock

Cook the rice in 4 cups of the water and 2 tsp of the salt for 1 hour. Set aside.

In a large skillet, cook the bacon over medium heat for 6–8 minutes, or until slightly crisp. Remove the bacon with a slotted spoon, reserve it and pour off all but a thin film of the fat from the skillet.

Add the onions and, stirring occasionally, cook 3–4 minutes, or until slightly translucent. Add the garlic and carrots and cook 5–6 minutes longer.

Return the reserved bacon to the skillet, stir in the vinegar, meat, the remaining 2 cups water, the remaining 1½ tsp salt, and a few grindings of black pepper. Reduce the heat to its lowest point and simmer, covered, for about 1 hour, or until the meat shows only a slight resistance when pierced with the tip of a small knife.

Stir in the cooked rice. Add the peppers and 1 cup of the beef stock. Bring to a boil, then cover and simmer 20 minutes, or until the rice is tender but not mushy. Season to taste. If at any point the rice becomes too dry or shows signs of sticking to the bottom of the pan, add remaining beef stock.

Hamburger Meatballs

I make these "hamburgers" with venison, rather than beef, and they are a hit every time. Serves 4–6.

2 slices stale whole wheat bread
¾ cup milk
1 lb minced venison *or* beef
1 egg, beaten
1 onion, finely chopped
1 tsp sea salt
¼ tsp freshly ground black pepper
½ cup whole wheat flour
2 tbsp meat drippings
½ cup water
2½ cups whole canned tomatoes
2 medium onions, sliced

Soak bread in milk for 1 hour until very soft. Mix meat, softened bread, egg, finely chopped onion, salt and pepper, and make into small meatballs. Roll in flour. Heat drippings in a skillet. When sizzling hot, put in floured meatballs and brown on all sides.

Preheat oven to 350°F. Remove meatballs to a large casserole. Pour the ½ cup water into the skillet and stir to dissolve browned juices, then pour over meatballs. Add tomatoes and sliced onion, and correct seasonings. Cover and simmer in oven for 2 hours. Reduce oven temperature to 325°F and simmer 1 hour longer.

Meat Loaf

This dish can be prepared with ground beef or game, and can be served at lunch or dinner. It is nutritious and delicious — and, when served on a silver platter, even elegant. I have had many requests for this recipe. Serves 4–6.

1 cup whole wheat bread crumbs
1 cup milk
2 lbs minced game *or* beef
1 onion, chopped
1 tsp sea salt
2 tsp Spike (available at health food stores)
1 tbsp prepared mustard
½ tsp sage
2 eggs
2 tbsp imitation bacon bits
½ cup tomato *or* vegetable juice

Preheat oven to 325°F. Soak crumbs in milk for 10 minutes. Add remaining ingredients, mix well and put in loaf pan. Pour juice over top and bake 1½–2 hours.

Short Ribs of Game or Beef

This excellent dish can be prepared ahead of time and baked just before a dinner party or, as we do at the lodge, served to guests and husband who can't tear themselves away from the river! You can use any kind of meat; we usually cook game, and very successfully. The recipe can be doubled. Serve the ribs with brown rice and a crisp green salad. Serves 4–6.

6 pieces short ribs
3 tbsp unbleached flour
1 tsp sea salt
⅛ tsp freshly ground black pepper
⅛ tsp paprika
2 tbsp sunflower oil
1 onion, chopped
2 tbsp brown sugar
1 cup water
½ tsp dry mustard
½ cup diced celery
¼ cup cider vinegar
2 tbsp soy sauce

Preheat the oven to 300°F. Cut the ribs into 3″ lengths. Combine the flour, salt, pepper and paprika. Rub the seasoned flour on the meat. Heat the oil in a skillet and sear the floured short ribs on all sides. Place the ribs in a casserole. Add the onion to the hot fat, cook and stir until golden brown. Add all remaining ingredients and heat to near boiling. Pour the sauce over the ribs. Cover tightly and bake until tender, about 2 hours.

Lamb Stew

This delectable dish takes very little time to prepare. You can assemble it a day ahead and keep it in the fridge. With freshly baked buns and a mixed salad, it is a superb meal for family and friends. Serves 4–6.

6 medium potatoes, peeled and cut crosswise
    into ¼" slices
4 large onions, peeled and cut into ¼" slices
3 lbs lean, boneless lamb (neck or shoulder),
    trimmed of all fat and cut into 1" cubes
1 tsp sea salt
freshly ground black pepper to taste
¼ tsp thyme
cold water

Spread half the potatoes on the bottom of a heavy 4- or 5-quart casserole or Dutch oven, cover with half the onion slices, then all of the lamb. Sprinkle with ½ tsp of the salt, a few grindings of pepper and the thyme. Arrange the rest of the onions over the meat and spread the remaining potatoes on top. Sprinkle with the remaining ½ tsp salt and a few grindings of pepper, then pour in just enough cold water to cover the potatoes.

Preheat the oven to 350°F. Bring the casserole to a boil on top of the stove, then bake for 1½ hours in the lower third of the oven.

Rice Casserole with Cheese

We have some guests and dear friends who are vegetarians. This casserole is nutritious and pleasing to all palates. Served with a salad, it is a filling and protein-rich main course. Serves 4–6.

2 cups brown rice
2 cups vegetable juice
2 cups water
1 tsp sea salt
1 tsp Spike (available at health food stores)
2 medium onions, chopped, *or* ¾ cup dried
    mixed vegetables
1 tsp honey *or* molasses
1 lb cheddar cheese, diced

In a medium pot, combine all ingredients *except* the cheese. Bring to a boil, stir, cover and simmer for 1¼ hours. Let stand 15 minutes before removing lid.

Preheat the oven to 350°F. Butter a casserole dish. Layer the rice and cheese alternately in the casserole, finishing with cheese. Bake about 20 minutes.

Transylvanian Goulash

This one is a great favourite in our house. Serves 4–6.

1 lb sauerkraut
2 tbsp lard
1 cup finely chopped onion
¼ tsp minced garlic
2 tbsp sweet Hungarian paprika
3 cups chicken stock
2 lbs boneless shoulder of pork, cut into 1″ cubes
1½ tsp caraway seeds
¼ cup tomato paste
½ cup sour cream
½ cup whipping cream
2 tbsp unbleached flour
sea salt to taste

Wash the sauerkraut thoroughly under cold running water and then soak it in cold water for 15 minutes. Melt the lard in a 5-quart casserole and add the onion. Cook over medium heat, stirring occasionally, for 6–8 minutes, or until golden. Add garlic and cook 1–2 minutes longer. Remove from heat, stir in paprika and continue to stir until the onions are well-coated. Pour in ½ cup of the stock and bring it to a boil, then add the pork.

Spread the sauerkraut over the pork and sprinkle it with the caraway seeds. In a small bowl, combine the tomato paste and the rest of the stock, and pour the mixture over the sauerkraut. Bring to a boil once more, then reduce the heat to its lowest point. Cover the casserole tightly and simmer 1 hour. Check every now and then to make sure the liquid has not cooked away. Add a little stock or water if it has; the sauerkraut should be moist.

When the pork is tender, combine the sour cream and whipping cream in a mixing bowl. Beat flour into cream with a wire whisk and carefully stir this mixture into the casserole. Simmer 10 minutes longer. Taste and correct seasonings. Add salt to taste. Serve the goulash in deep individual plates, accompanied by a bowl of sour cream.

Venison and Mushroom Casserole

This is a marvellous dish when one isn't sure at which point the hungry hunters or fishermen will return to the herd. It is also a great "cook-ahead" for a dinner party. Serves 4–6.

2 lbs venison
1 tsp sea salt
¼ tsp freshly ground black pepper
¼ tsp oregano
¼ tsp garlic powder
1 medium onion, sliced
3 tbsp olive oil
1½ cups water
2 cups sliced mushrooms (fresh, frozen or canned)
1 can mushroom soup

Cut venison into 2″ cubes, put in a large bowl and sprinkle with salt, pepper, oregano and garlic powder. Brown meat and onion in the oil. Add water, cover and simmer gently until meat is tender (2–2½ hours).

Preheat oven to 350°F. Turn the mixture into a casserole and add mushrooms and mushroom soup. Mix well. Bake 35 minutes.

Schnitz un Knepp

One year I had to accompany two of Walter's clients on a hunt to the Chilcotin country. We were guests of Alfred Bryan, a guide-outfitter who owned a ranch deep in the Rainbow Mountains. Alfred and Johnny Root, a Pennsylvania Dutch man, took care of us for ten unforgettable days. We spent most of our time on horseback in a beautiful, pristine, ever-changing countryside. After eight hours in the saddle, the Europeans and I were only capable of dismounting before we collapsed. Johnny, meanwhile, would either hustle off to his stove in a cabin or start an open fire outside. And after what seemed only a short while, he would ring the gong and shout, "Come, come, come!!" He would be dressed in a white shirt, have the table set invitingly, and produce the most delicious fare. Never before or since have I eaten anything like it. Served in a tent, with a fierce snowstorm blowing, and Woolworth's glasses sparkling in the candlelight to match the brilliance of the snow crystals outside, the meal became a feast. Serves 6.

    4 cups dried apples
    3 lbs ham
    2 tbsp brown sugar (use 1 tbsp if the apples are
        very sweet)
    Classic Dumplings (see p. 71)

Wash apples, cover with water and soak overnight. Also cook ham that night by covering with cold water and simmering for 3 hours. In the morning, add the apples and soaking water, and simmer 1 hour longer. Add brown sugar.

In the evening, bring the ham to a boil again. During the last few minutes of cooking time, drop in dumplings.

Deer Liver Pâté

Here is a perfect cold cut or sandwich filling. You can also serve it as an appetizer—if you do, just omit the flour sauce. Serves 4–6.

1½ lbs deer liver
1½ cups boiling water
4 slices bacon
1 small onion, chopped
2 cups bread crumbs (best if made from
    homemade bread)
¼ cup chopped fresh parsley
2 eggs, slightly beaten
1 tsp sea salt
¼ tsp freshly ground black pepper
2 tbsp unbleached flour
1½ cups cold water

Rinse liver well, cover with the boiling water and let stand 15 minutes. Drain. Put liver and bacon through a meat grinder, then add onion, bread crumbs, parsley, eggs, salt and pepper. Mix well.

Preheat oven to 350°F. Press pâté into an 8" x 4" loaf pan. Bake 1 hour or until browned. Remove loaf to a hot platter, leaving sauce in the pan. Mix flour with a bit of the cold water, stir into the sauce and cook on top of the stove until brown. Add remaining water gradually, and cook 5 minutes longer or until thickened. Season to taste and pour over loaf.

Rabbit Casserole with Dumplings

For some years we have been fortunate to sample Mary Banks's superb cooking in Victoria. On one visit, she served us this rabbit casserole. I happened to mention that I hadn't had rabbit since leaving East Germany, and now this delicious meal awaits us on each of our annual visits to Mary. She has very kindly parted with her recipe. "One evening," she says, "I had a long distance call from my younger son in Rocky Mountain House, asking how to cook a rabbit. Six calls later the rabbit had got out of its skin and onto the table. At least I did not have to catch it first. I thought I had better write the recipe down for posterity."

Buy whole rabbits, because they are easy to disjoint. Take the forelegs off with the shoulder blade included, and the back legs at the hips. Cut the back into three. If the rabbits are already cut up, you may want to make the pieces smaller.

A little leftover rabbit makes a delicious soup for lunch on a cold day. Just add a can of consommé, a dessert-spoonful of red currant jelly, and some sherry. Bring to a boil. Remove bones before serving and sprinkle with parsley.

One rabbit serves 4 people.

¼ lb salt pork
cooking oil (optional)
1 rabbit, cut up
unbleached flour
2 onions
4 carrots
bouquet garni (mixed herbs tied in a little
    cheesecloth bag)

½ cup sliced mushrooms (optional)
2 cups fresh or canned chicken stock *or* water
2 tbsp white *or* red wine to taste
Bread Crumb Dumplings (see p. 70)
Beurre Manié (see p. 70)

Remove rind from pork. Dice pork into ½″ cubes. Sauté gently in a skillet until golden brown, adding a little cooking oil if needed. Remove to casserole.

Roll the rabbit in flour; do not salt (the pork provides sufficient salt). Sauté until slightly brown and add to casserole. (I also add the rabbit kidneys, but not the liver—it is a trifle strong.)

Chop the onions into quarters or eighths. Sauté until slightly brown and a little soft. Slice the carrots and add to casserole with bouquet garni and sliced mushrooms. Add a little flour to absorb any fat left in the skillet and make a sauce by stirring in hot stock or water. Pour sauce over rabbit and add cold liquid to cover, plus a good dollop of wine.

Preheat oven to 325°F. Bake casserole until it comes to a boil. Reduce heat and simmer 1½ hours, or until tender but not quite falling away from the bone. Correct seasonings and put the meat in a large dish to keep warm. Bring the liquid to a boil and drop in dumplings, making sure they are completely covered. Bake in oven for 7–10 minutes. When done, the dumplings should have doubled in size and floated to the top. Test with a sharp knife—if they feel sticky, cook a little more. Arrange dumplings around the rabbit. Thicken the sauce with Beurre Manié (see p. 70) if necessary. Pour some sauce and vegetables over the rabbit and serve the rest of the sauce in a gravy boat. Red currant jelly is a pleasant accompaniment.

Beurre Manié

Beat together equal quantities of butter and flour until creamy. (For the Rabbit Casserole, start with 1½ tbsp each.) Stir into simmering liquid, and cook about 5 minutes. Leftover Beurre Manié will store well in the fridge for up to 2 weeks, and can be used for any sauce.

Bread Crumb Dumplings

Serves 6.

  1–1¼ cups unbleached flour
  1–1¼ cups soft white bread crumbs (homemade or home style)
  ½–¾ cup ground suet
  2 heaping tsp baking powder

Mix all ingredients with just enough cold water to make a stiff dough: it should be wet enough to absorb all the dry ingredients, but not wet enough to wring out! Form into small apricot-sized balls. Roll in flour and cook as directed above.

Classic Dumplings

2 cups unbleached flour, sifted
1 tsp sea salt
4 tsp baking powder
1 egg, well beaten
3 tbsp unsalted butter, melted
⅔ cup milk (approx.)

Sift dry ingredients together; add egg and butter. Carefully pour in milk, a little at a time, just until the batter is moist-stiff. Drop by spoonfuls into boiling Schnitz un Knepp (p. 66) or other stew. Cover tightly and cook 20 minutes over medium heat. Serve piping hot.

Feather Dumplings

Everyone loves dumplings with stew, and this light-as-a-feather version is guaranteed to please. Serves 4–6.

2 cups sifted whole wheat flour *or* unbleached
   flour
1 tsp sea salt
4 tsp baking powder
⅔ cup milk
1 egg, well beaten
3 tbsp olive oil
⅛ tsp pepper

Sift dry ingredients twice. Add milk, egg, oil and pepper. Mix just until all ingredients are blended. Drop by teaspoons into boiling liquid. Cover tightly and cook 18 minutes.

Cream of Wheat Dumplings

In Austria, dumplings are great favourites. There are many different varieties for many different occasions. These dumplings are very versatile — wonderful with soup, or as a delectable dessert served with preserved fruit or jam. Serves 4–6.

1 egg
3½ tbsp unsalted butter
⅔ cup cream of wheat
milk (optional)

Beat egg into butter and add cream of wheat. Let stand at least 30 minutes. Form into small balls, 1″ in diameter. Add to simmering liquid, cover tightly and simmer 15 minutes without lifting the lid.

For dessert dumplings, add dough balls to boiling water or milk. Turn off heat, cover tightly and let stand at least 15 minutes without lifting the lid.

Potato Dumplings

Another one from Grandmother's kitchen. Serves 4–6.

5 medium potatoes, unpeeled
5 quarts water
⅓ cup unbleached flour
1 tsp sea salt
¼ cup farina
2 tsp milk
1 egg, lightly beaten

Start in the morning. Boil the potatoes; cool and peel. Rice the potato (you should have about 2¾ cups).

Boil the water in a large saucepan. In a bowl, combine the remaining ingredients and the potato, and beat with a wooden spoon until smooth. Dust your hands with flour and form dough into small balls 1–2" in diameter.

Drop dumplings into the boiling water and bring to a gentle boil. Simmer, uncovered, until dumplings rise to the top (about 10 minutes).

Venison Jerky

This recipe was given to me by an outdoorsman in Montana, who is an excellent wild game cook. Makes 2–3 dozen jerky strips.

2 lbs venison
2 cups table salt
5–6 cups water
¼ cup sugar
2 bottles liquid smoke

Slice venison into thin strips. Remove all fat.

Combine remaining ingredients and bring to a boil to make brine. While still boiling, drop in a few pieces of venison at a time and cook 30 seconds, just until it turns colour. Dry in a slow oven (90–100°F) for at least 1 day, or dry on racks in the sun.

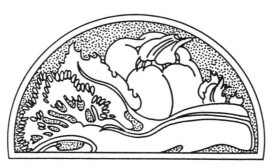

Salads, Dressings,
Vegetables

Our Own Rotkraut Salat

This salad is not only good and good for you, it can also be served with almost anything at any time. It has always been a great success with our guests. Serves 4–6.

1 small head red cabbage, shredded
1 tsp sea salt
1 tbsp lemon juice
2–3 tsp liquid honey
1–2 tbsp olive oil
1 apple, chopped
¼ onion, finely chopped

Combine cabbage and salt and let stand 20 minutes. Press out excess liquid. Mix in lemon juice, honey, oil, apple and onion.

Copper Bay Cole Slaw

Here is the sister to Our Own Rotkraut Salat—a simple, scrumptious cole slaw. Serve it with any meal. Even during the wintertime, when we have great difficulty obtaining tasty fresh vegetables, I am always able to get organically grown carrots and cabbage (both red and green). Serves 4–6.

1 small head green cabbage, shredded
½ cup Our Favourite Mayonnaise (see p. 86)
½ cup raisins
½ cup shredded carrot
1 apple, finely chopped

Mix all ingredients well and chill.

Oriental Cole Slaw

Viola Isbister, who created this recipe, moved to Queen Charlotte City in 1982 to help her sister and brother-in-law with their grocery store. Now she works at a flower and craft store, doing what she loves best — tending and arranging flowers. All of us consider it a special treat when Viola presents us with one of her beautiful bouquets, or when she prepares this salad, her creation and the most famous cole slaw on the Queen Charlotte Islands! Whenever you serve it, you should have several "handouts" ready, so great is the demand for this recipe. Serves 10–12.

Oriental Cole Slaw Dressing:
1 pkt Ichiban seasoning
6 tbsp vinegar
1 cup oil
½ cup sugar

1 large head green cabbage, cut very fine but not grated
4 green onions, sliced
1 cup toasted, slivered almonds
½ cup toasted sesame seeds
1 pkg Ichiban soup noodles (chicken or vegetable flavour), crumbled

Prepare Oriental Cole Slaw Dressing by combining all ingredients thoroughly. Combine the cabbage and green onions. Just before serving, add almonds, sesame seeds and noodles. Toss well with the dressing.

Tomato Salad

Serves 4-6.

5-6 medium firm tomatoes
½ cup olive oil
2 tbsp cider vinegar *or* lemon juice
1 tsp basil
½-1 tsp sea salt
1-2 cloves garlic, crushed
freshly ground black pepper to taste
2 tbsp chives
1 tbsp chopped fresh parsley

Slice tomatoes and arrange on a large platter. Combine all other ingredients, *except* chives and parsley. Pour dressing over tomatoes, and sprinkle with chives and parsley.

Copper Bay Potato Salad

I have passed on this recipe for potato salad to many guests who claim they have never eaten a better salad. We serve the dish with baked or steamed coho or steelhead, and hot brown rice. My husband maintains that this unusual combination flavours and textures is the ultimate in eating. Bon appétit! Serves 4–6.

Potato Salad Dressing (see p. 86)
7–8 medium potatoes (organically grown are
    best)
¼–½ cup hot chicken stock
1 tsp dill weed
1 tbsp imitation bacon bits
½ cup chopped green onion
2 eggs, hard-boiled and chopped (optional)

Prepare the Potato Salad Dressing.

Cook potatoes in their skins. Peel while still warm. Pour the stock and salad dressing over the potatoes, but *do not stir*! Gently fold in the rest of the ingredients.

Salami Salad

Serves 4–6.

4 oz sliced salami
1 head iceberg lettuce, cut into wedges
½ cucumber, sliced
4 oz gruyere cheese, sliced thin
1 bunch watercress, trimmed
1 clove garlic, crushed
1 tsp Dijon mustard
6 tbsp olive oil
2 tbsp cider vinegar
freshly ground black pepper to taste
¼ tsp sea salt
4 oz cheddar cheese, cut into ¼″ cubes
radishes

On 8 slices of salami, make a cut from outside edge to centre. Shape into cones and arrange on one side of a large serving plate. Cut the remaining salami into thin strips. Arrange the lettuce, cucumber, gruyere cheese and watercress on the other side of the plate. Prepare the dressing by mixing together the garlic, mustard, oil, vinegar, pepper and salt. Pile the cheddar cheese, radishes and salami strips in the centre of the plate and pour a little dressing over. Pour the rest of the dressing over the lettuce and cucumber. Serve at once.

Nutty Sprout and Carrot Salad

Serves 4.

6 tbsp olive oil
2 tbsp cider vinegar
grated rind and juice of ½ orange
½–1 tsp prepared mustard (coarse is best)
pinch brown sugar
freshly ground black pepper to taste
½ tsp sea salt
4 tbsp toasted hazelnuts *or* walnuts
½ cup sprouts
½ cup scraped and grated carrot
2 tbsp raisins
chicory leaves

To make the dressing, blend together the oil, vinegar, orange rind and juice, mustard, sugar, pepper and salt. Mix well. Chop 1 tbsp of the nuts finely and add to dressing. Halve the remaining nuts and place in a bowl with the sprouts, carrot and raisins. Pour dressing over and toss well. Garnish with chicory leaves.

Our Favourite Salad Dressing

A lady who used to live in Sandspit supplied me with a recipe for a wonderful salad dressing, but it called for some ingredients we do not use. As we avoid white sugar, commercial ketchup and white vinegar, we remodelled the recipe to our specifications. Since then, we have earned only praise from those who have tasted it. Makes 1 cup.

    2 tbsp brown sugar or honey
    1 tsp sea salt
    ½ tsp dry mustard
    ½ tsp paprika
    ½ tsp oregano
    ½ tsp garlic salt
    ¼ cup finely chopped onion
    ½ cup cider vinegar
    ½ cup ketchup (homemade or bought from a
        health food store)
    ½ cup sunflower oil

Combine dry ingredients in a jar with a tight-fitting lid. Add remaining ingredients. Shake vigorously. Chill. Serve on salad greens, sliced tomatoes, or bean salad.

Our Favourite Mayonnaise

The secret of a successful homemade mayonnaise is simply to have the ingredients at room temperature. Makes 1¼ cups.

  1 egg
  ⅛ tsp cayenne
  ½ tsp sea salt
  ½ tsp dry mustard
  1 tsp honey
  1 cup olive oil
  2 tbsp lemon juice

Combine egg, cayenne, salt, mustard, honey and ¼ cup of the oil in a blender. Cover and blend on low speed until well mixed. When the mayonnaise thickens, add the lemon juice and, while blending, slowly pour in the rest of the oil.

Potato Salad Dressing

Makes ½–¾ cup.

  ½ small onion, coarsely chopped
  3 tsp cider vinegar
  ½ tsp sea salt
  ½ tsp freshly ground black pepper
  2 tsp prepared mustard
  ½ cup sunflower oil *or* olive oil

Blend the first 5 ingredients together in a blender at high speed for about 10 seconds, then turn blender to low speed and slowly add the oil.

Horseradish Cream Dressing

Makes ½–¾ cup.

½ cup whipping cream
1 tbsp cider vinegar
1 tsp light brown sugar
¼ tsp sea salt
2 tbsp grated horseradish

Whip the cream and fold in the rest of the ingredients gently.

Copper Bay Salad Dressing

Makes 2 cups.

2 eggs
1 large can evaporated milk
1 tsp prepared mustard
1 tsp sea salt
1 tsp brown sugar
½ cup cider vinegar *or* lemon juice

Beat eggs until light and creamy. Add milk and beat well again. Mix together the mustard, salt and sugar and add to egg mixture. Then beat in the vinegar or lemon juice. Keep in a covered jar in the refrigerator.

Fruit Salad Dressing

Makes 1⅔ cups.

3 tbsp arrowroot powder *or* cornstarch
¾ cup light brown sugar
¼ tsp sea salt
2 eggs, slightly beaten
½ cup pineapple juice
⅓ cup lemon juice
¼ cup unsalted butter
½ cup whipped cream

Blend arrowroot powder, sugar and salt in the top of a double boiler. Add eggs, pineapple juice and lemon juice. Cook over hot water until thick. Add butter, and cool. Fold in whipped cream.

Sour Cream or Yogurt Salad Dressing

Use this creamy sauce as a dressing for fresh cucumbers or Boston lettuce. Makes 1¼ cups.

1 cup sour cream *or* yogurt
2 tsp warmed honey
2 tbsp lemon juice
1 tsp sea salt
freshly ground black pepper to taste

Pour the sour cream into a bowl. Slowly stir in honey. When absorbed, add lemon juice, salt and pepper. Beat until well blended.

Grandmother's Red Cabbage

Cabbages grew in abundance in our garden when I was a child, and they were served throughout the long winter months in many different ways. The following recipe was very popular in my grandmother's house. Adults and children alike loved it; we even accepted that the dish would "ward off colds." Numerous guests at Copper Bay have exclaimed, "It tastes just like my mother's!" Delicious with any meat, particularly game. Serves 4–6.

2–2½ lbs red cabbage
⅔ cup cider vinegar
2 tbsp brown sugar
2 tsp sea salt
2 tbsp lard *or* oil
2 medium apples, peeled, cored and cut into ⅛"
 wedges
½ cup finely chopped onion
1 whole onion, peeled and pierced with 2 whole
 cloves
1 small bay leaf
5 cups boiling water
3 tbsp dry red wine (optional)

Wash the cabbage, remove tough outer leaves and cut into quarters. Cut out the core and shred cabbage by slicing the quarters crosswise into ⅛" strips.

In a large mixing bowl, sprinkle vinegar, sugar and salt over the cabbage. Toss with a spoon to coat evenly. In a heavy 4- to 5-quart casserole, heat the lard or oil over medium heat. Add apples and chopped onion and cook, stirring frequently, for 5 minutes or until the apples are lightly browned. Add the cabbage, the whole onion with cloves, and the bay leaf; stir thoroughly and pour the boiling water over all. Bring to a boil over high heat, stirring occasionally, then reduce the heat to its lowest possible point. Cover and simmer 1½–2 hours or until the cabbage is tender. Check from time to time to ensure that the cabbage is moist. If needed, add 1 tbsp boiling water.

Before serving, remove whole onion and bay leaf, and stir in wine if desired. Transfer to a warm bowl and serve.

Italian-Style Broccoli or Cauliflower

We are very fond of broccoli and cauliflower, so I was quite pleased when the following recipe was given to me by a superb "veggy-cook." Serves 4.

1 lb broccoli or cauliflower
3 tsp olive oil
2 cloves garlic, minced
freshly ground black pepper to taste
sea salt to taste
chopped fresh parsley to taste

Break the broccoli or cauliflower into small florets and cut the stems into small pieces. Boil gently in salted water for 5–6 minutes. The pieces must be slightly undercooked. Drain well.

Heat the olive oil in a skillet. Add the garlic and let it brown, then add vegetables and cook 5 minutes. Add pepper and salt to taste. Sprinkle with chopped parsley.

Glazed Onions

Here is another recipe from Scotland. It makes a perfect side dish for any main course. Serves 4–6.

12 small (about 1½″) boiling onions
4 tbsp unsalted butter
2 tbsp honey
½ tsp sea salt

Preheat the oven to 400°F. Drop the onions into boiling water (they must be immersed). Cook briskly, uncovered, for 1–2 minutes. Drain in a colander. With a sharp knife, trim the stem ends, remove the parchment-like skins, and cut off the tops. Arrange in an attractive baking dish large enough to hold the onions comfortably in one layer. Melt the butter over medium heat. When the foam starts to subside, add honey and salt. Stir until mixture is fluid. Pour over onions; turn them with a spoon to coat evenly. Bake the onions 45 minutes or until golden brown, basting every 10 minutes with the cooking liquid. Serve at once, directly from the baking dish.

Honey Glazed Carrots

Parsnips and yellow or white turnips are excellent substitutes for the carrots in this recipe. Serves 4–6.

12 medium carrots, scraped and cut into 2″
    chunks
1½ cups chicken stock
4 tbsp unsalted butter
2 tbsp honey
½ tsp sea salt
freshly ground black pepper to taste
2 tbsp finely chopped chives *or* parsley

Bring carrots to a boil in chicken stock, butter, honey, salt and pepper over medium heat. Cover and simmer about 20 minutes. Shake the skillet a few times and check that the liquid does not cook away too quickly. Should the stock not reduce during cooking time, remove the carrots and reduce liquid by boiling a few minutes over high heat. Coat the carrots by rolling them around the pan. Transfer to a warmed serving dish and sprinkle with chives or parsley.

Sour Cream Summer Squash

I don't remember who supplied me with this recipe, but whoever it was, thank you! Serves 6.

3 tbsp margarine
1 onion, sliced
2 lbs yellow squash, sliced
1 cup thick sour cream
sea salt to taste
freshly ground black pepper to taste
paprika to taste

Heat margarine in a skillet and sauté onion about 5 minutes, or until soft. Add sliced squash and continue cooking until lightly browned. Add sour cream and simmer until squash is tender. Season to taste and sprinkle with paprika.

Potatoes Au Gratin

Serves 4–6.

5–6 unpeeled potatoes
2 cups White Sauce (see p. 38)
¼ tsp onion salt *or* 1 tsp grated onion
2 cups grated Rat Trap cheese *or* extra-old white
    cheddar cheese
sea salt to taste
½ cup whole wheat bread crumbs

Cook potatoes in salted water. Cool, peel and cut into small cubes. Add white sauce, onion salt and half the grated cheese. Add sea salt if necessary.

Preheat oven to 325°F. Place in attractive, buttered baking dish. Sprinkle crumbs and remaining cheese on top. Bake 30 minutes or until cheese is melted and slightly browned.

Fried Potato Patties

Serve these patties as an accompaniment to a roast, or with a sweetened fruit. As children, we adored them; my daughters were in rapture when either of their grannies prepared them for the evening meal. Serves 8–10.

6 medium potatoes, unpeeled
1 egg
2 tsp sea salt
½–¾ cup unbleached flour
5 tbsp butter (approx.)

Boil potatoes just until tender. Drain and cool. Force cold potatoes through a ricer. Beat in egg, salt and ½ cup of the flour. Beat vigorously until the mixture is smooth and dense enough to hold its shape. If it is too soft, beat in remaining flour, a tablespoon at a time. Flour your hands and make individual patties 3–4" in diameter. Melt 2 tbsp of the butter in a heavy 10"–12" skillet over high heat. When the foam has subsided, add as many patties as the skillet holds comfortably, and brown them 3–5 minutes on each side, turning carefully with a large spatula. Transfer to warmed serving platter and cover loosely with foil while you cook the rest. Add more butter as needed.

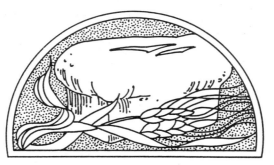

Breads and Rolls

Sourdough Rye Bread

The recipe for these wonderful loaves comes from our Public Health Nurse, Kathryn Kelly, who provided me with my first sourdough starter. Makes 3 loaves.

1 cup Sourdough Starter (see p. 102)
6 cups warm water
10 cups flour (I use 7 cups rye, 2 whole wheat, 1
    unbleached)
½ cup molasses
2 tbsp salt
1 cup milk (optional)

Combine starter, water, 5 cups rye flour and 1 cup unbleached flour. Mix well. Cover and let stand overnight.

In the morning, take out 1 cup of dough and refrigerate (it is your next batch of starter). Combine remaining ingredients. Knead thoroughly. Shape into loaves and let rise 3–6 hours.

Preheat oven to 325°F. Bake 1½–2 hours.

Sourdough White and Raisin Bread

When our daughter Andrea comes home with her children, one of her first questions is, "Do you have a loaf of the delicious sourdough raisin bread?" This is perfect for toast or Cinnamon Toast (see p. 111). Makes 2 small loaves.

> 6 ½ cups unbleached flour
> 2 cups lukewarm water
> 1 cup Sourdough Starter (see p. 102)
> 1 tsp sea salt
> 3 tbsp liquid honey *or* maple syrup
> ½ tsp baking soda
> 3 tbsp sunflower oil
> 1 cup raisins (optional)
> 1 cup chopped nuts (your choice; optional)

The night before baking, add 2½ cups of the flour and the lukewarm water to 1 cup of sourdough starter. Beat well until smooth. Cover and set in a warm place overnight. In the morning, take out 1 cup of sourdough for your new starter. To the rest of the dough, add the remaining 4 cups flour, the salt, honey, baking soda and oil. Mix thoroughly. Add raisins and nuts.

As soon as the dough has a suitable consistency for kneading, turn it out on a well-floured board and knead until satiny and smooth (about 10–12 minutes). Put dough in a well-greased bowl, turn to grease all sides, cover with a towel and set in a warm place to rise for about 2½ hours. Punch down and shape into 2 small loaves. Place in well-greased, warm loaf pans and let rise about 1 hour.

Preheat oven to 375°F. Bake bread ¾–1 hour, or until golden brown.

Sourdough Pancakes

Breakfast is the most important meal to Natasha, our young and very small granddaughter. As that is when Tash's appetite seems to be the largest, we try to make breakfast as delicious, nutritious and colourful as possible. However, her most frequent request is for our sourdough pancakes with maple syrup and sweet butter. Serves 4–6.

2 cups lukewarm water
2½ cups unbleached flour
1 cup Sourdough Starter (see p. 102)
2 eggs
2 tbsp oil
¼–½ cup evaporated milk (enough to make a
   pourable batter)
1 tsp sea salt
1 tsp baking soda
2 tbsp brown sugar

The night before, add the water and flour to the sourdough pot. Beat until smooth, cover and set in a warm place overnight. In the morning, stir the dough down and take out 1 cup of it for your sourdough pot. Add the eggs, oil and milk to the remaining dough. Beat until smooth.

In a small bowl, combine the sea salt, baking soda and brown sugar. Blend until no baking soda lumps are left. Sprinkle evenly over sourdough batter, then mix together gently. Letter batter rest 10–15 minutes. Fry pancakes on a *hot*, lightly greased griddle or skillet. Serve at once.

Sourdough Starter

Almost every sourdough pot has a story attached to it and can proudly present a long and distinguished lineage. My starter came from our Public Health Nurse, Kathryn Kelly, who financed her post-grad studies by working in a bakery during the very early hours of the morning. By the time she received her BA in nursing, she was also a very accomplished baker. The transaction took place many years ago, but the "pot" is "alive and well" and has a permanent place in the back of our fridge. We have been away from Copper Bay for months at a time, only to come back to an eager and ready "pot," and our delicious sourdough goodies. Should your "pot" look a bit tired after having been neglected for some time, stir in 1–2 tbsp flour the day before your baking day. Makes 2 cups.

¼ pkg active dry yeast
1½ cups tepid water
2 cups flour (any type, any combination)

In a large bowl or jar, mix the yeast and water. Let it stand for about 10 minutes. Sprinkle flour into yeast mixture and whisk it in to form a thick batter. Cover with plastic wrap and let batter stand in a warm (80–85°F) place for 24 hours or until frothy. The starter can be used at once but will have a richer flavour if left in a warm place for 3 days longer.

Starter that is not used immediately should be covered tightly with plastic wrap or poured into a 1-quart Mason jar with a tight lid, and refrigerated. The starter will keep in the fridge for up to 2 weeks. Before using it, leave it at room temperature and stir well before removing the amount required.

It is very important that after each use, the starter "pot" is replenished with an equal amount of the flour and water mixture prepared the evening before the baking day.

Yeasted Rye Bread

Makes 2 loaves.

3 cups rye flour
1 cup muesli
2½ tbsp honey
¼ cup olive oil
1 tbsp sea salt
1 tbsp lecithin granules
1 tbsp Fermipan yeast
2¼ cups lukewarm water

Combine flour, muesli, honey, oil, salt, lecithin and yeast in a large bowl. Add water and mix in a mixer at low speed for 2 minutes, or beat vigorously by hand. Turn onto a lightly floured kneading board and knead 5–10 minutes, until the dough feels smooth and elastic. Place dough in an oiled bowl and turn once so that all sides are greased. Cover and let rise in a warm place until double in size (about 1¼ hours). Punch down and form into 2 balls. Cover and let stand about 15 minutes.

Form dough into 2 loaves and make a few diagonal slashes across the top of each loaf. Let rise 30–45 minutes, or until double in size.

Preheat oven to 375°F. Bake bread 50–55 minutes.

Copper Bay Bread

After we arrived on the Islands, our daughters were determined to make a cook out of their mother and felt we had to start baking our own bread. The first loaves were disastrous, especially as we had an electric stove with one element only (the bottom one). However, after a period of upset stomachs, our health and the quality of our bread improved, and we now bake loaves that are entirely our own creation. I have had to copy out the following recipe numerous times. In fact, the many requests for it first gave me the idea to put together a cookbook with all of our favourite foods. Makes 3 loaves.

4 cups lukewarm water *or* 2 cups water + 2 cups scalded milk
4 tbsp molasses
1 tbsp active dry yeast
4 cups whole wheat flour *or* graham flour
2½ tsp dulse salt *or* sea salt
¼ cup oil
½ cup sunflower seeds
½ cup soy flakes
1 tbsp soy flour
1 tbsp bran
1 tbsp brewer's yeast
1 tbsp wheat germ
1 tbsp lecithin granules
1 tsp dulse powder (if sea salt was used above)
1 tsp whey powder
about 5 cups unbleached flour (enough to make a soft dough)

Combine all ingredients and beat well. I use my food

processor with great success. Knead thoroughly, about 10 minutes. Cover and let rise in a warm place for 1½ hours or until double in bulk. Punch down, divide into 3 equal parts and sprinkle with bran. Let rise ½–1 hour.

Preheat oven to 375°F. Bake bread 65–70 minutes.

Sweet Rolls

Although these rolls are made with honey or maple syrup, we often serve them for dinner and warm up any leftovers for breakfast the next morning. When our children were young, they asked to add raisins to the dough; then we all enjoyed them for tea. Makes 24.

    1 tbsp active dry yeast
    1 tsp brown sugar
    ½ cup warm water
    2 tbsp sunflower oil
    2 tbsp honey *or* maple syrup
    1 tsp salt
    2 cups boiling water
    2 eggs, beaten
    unbleached white flour
    1 cup raisins (optional)

Combine the yeast, brown sugar and warm water in a bowl and let the mixture sit until it foams to the top (about 10 minutes). In a separate large bowl, combine the oil, honey, salt and boiling water until all ingredients are dissolved, then cool to lukewarm. Add yeast mixture, eggs, flour and raisins. The dough should be kneaded but not stiff. Cover and let rise until at least triple in bulk.

Form dough into rolls of desired shapes and place in muffin tins or 1″ apart on greased baking sheet. Let rise until double in bulk.

Preheat oven to 350°F. Bake 30 minutes.

Bagels

This recipe comes from Macey Cadesky, a gifted musician who has played with the Toronto Symphony Orchestra. Not long after he and his wife Rosalie came to the Queen Charlottes, he had most of the community singing in a choir or learning piano or violin, and Rosalie's talents were in big demand at the local school, where she worked with children with special needs. Macey is also a very accomplished cook, and before he and Rosalie moved off the islands, he presented me with this recipe.

2 cups warm water
2 tbsp active dry yeast
2 tsp + 2 tbsp brown sugar
¼ cup vegetable or corn oil
1 tbsp salt
5 ½ cups unbleached flour (approx.)
corn meal
poppy seeds (optional)
coarse salt (optional)

Combine the warm water, yeast and 2 tsp of the sugar. Let stand 5–10 minutes. Transfer to large mixing bowl. Whisk to separate yeast. Add oil and salt. Add flour a little at a time, and whisk to mix. When thick, gradually add remaining flour, stirring with a mixing spoon. Transfer dough to kneading surface, adding flour and kneading to make a stiff dough. Let rise in an oiled bowl until double in bulk. Punch down.

Make ropes of dough as thick as your finger, and cut into 6"–8" lengths. Overlap ends and roll to join dough into bagel shape. Grease cookie sheet with margarine and set bagels on sheet to rise slightly. Add the remaining 2 tbsp sugar to a large pot of water and bring to simmering. Place bagels, a few at a time, in simmering water. Cook 3–4 minutes on each side.

Preheat oven to 400°F. Transfer bagels to another cookie sheet which has been greased with margarine and sprinkled with corn meal or flour. Sprinkle bagels with poppy seeds and coarse salt if desired. Bake 20 minutes or until golden brown.

Variations:
1. Use 1½ cups rye flour and remainder unbleached or all-purpose flour.
2. Add 1 tsp caraway seeds to dough.
3. Sprinkle caraway seeds on bagels before baking.

Scones

1 egg, separated
3 cups unbleached flour
2 tsp baking powder
½ cup unsalted butter, softened
1 cup brown sugar
1 cup milk
1 cup chopped raisins *or* apricots

Preheat oven to 400°F. Beat egg white until stiff. In a separate bowl, mix together, in this order, the flour, baking powder, butter, brown sugar and milk. Fold in fruit and beaten egg white. Roll dough ½″ thick and spread with the egg yolk. Cut into squares or triangles. Bake about 15 minutes.

Bran Muffins

Everybody seems to have become aware that the North American diet needs more fibre, and quite a few Copper Bay Lodge guests have exchanged the traditional breakfast of bacon and eggs for a wholesome grain-cum-bran muffin morningfest. Here is one of my favourite bran muffin recipes. Makes 12.

1 cup unbleached flour (organic is best)
½ cup whole wheat flour
½ tsp sea salt
1½ tsp baking soda
1½ cups bran
1 tsp cinnamon
½ tsp nutmeg
1½ cups milk
2 tbsp lemon juice
¼ cup molasses
⅓ cup honey
2 eggs, slightly beaten
¼ cup oil
1 cup grated carrot (organic, unpeeled)
½ cup chopped dates *or* raisins
½ cup chopped almonds

Mix dry ingredients in one bowl. Mix liquid ingredients with carrots, fruit and nuts in another bowl. Combine the two mixtures just until the dry ingredients are moistened. Do not overbeat.

Preheat oven to 375°F. Fill greased muffin tins two-thirds full. Bake 20 minutes.

Maple Bran Muffins

Makes 8–10 muffins.

1½ cups bran *or* 9-grain cereal
1 cup buttermilk *or* sour milk (1 cup milk
    combined with 1 tbsp cider vinegar or lemon
    juice, and allowed to thicken)
½ cup maple syrup
1 egg
⅓ cup olive oil
½ tsp vanilla
1 cup unbleached flour
½ tsp sea salt
1 tsp baking soda
1 tsp baking powder
½ cup mashed banana (optional)
½ cup currants, raisins *or* dates

Mix bran and buttermilk and let stand 10 minutes.

Preheat oven to 375°F. Combine maple syrup, egg, oil and vanilla, then add to bran mixture. Sift together flour, salt, baking soda and baking powder and add to bran mixture. Add fruit, and stir just until the dry ingredients are moistened. Do not overbeat.

Fill greased muffin cups two-thirds full. Bake 15–20 minutes.

Cinnamon Toast

There is nothing cozier than a tea in front of a roaring fire, especially when a fierce Southeast is blowing and the children have to stay indoors. Cinnamon toast produces not only hearty appetites but lots of smiles and exclamations! It is a great reward for very little effort. Makes enough for 4–6 slices.

Stir together 3 tbsp brown sugar and 1 tsp cinnamon in a cup. Sprinkle over hot buttered toast and cut toast into strips and triangles. For best results, use sourdough white bread for the toast.

Three-Fruit Marmalade

If you can't get bitter oranges, use navel oranges for this delectable marmalade. Try to get organically grown fruit – it makes all the difference. Makes 8–10 cups.

    2 bitter oranges
    5 navel oranges
    1 lemon
    1 grapefruit
    2 quarts water
    light brown sugar

Day 1: Wash fruit and dry well. Cut into quarters and cut each quarter into fine strips. Pour water over the fruit and let stand overnight.
Day 2: Cook the fruit at a low boil for 25 minutes.
Day 3: Mix 2 cups light brown sugar for each 1 quart

cooked fruit (you will have about 2 quarts) into the fruit and boil 20 minutes, stirring constantly. Fill sterilized jars while mixture is still hot; seal and store.

Lemon Cheese

Serve this tart-sweet spread on toast, buns or bread. Just right for breakfast or tea-time. Makes 1½ cups.

2 cups sugar
½ cup butter
juice of 3 lemons
grated rind of 2 lemons
5 eggs

Stir all ingredients together in a double boiler and cook at a light boil until creamy.

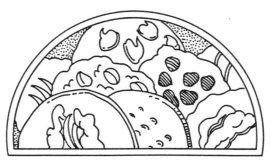

Cookies

Nut Cookies

These cookies can be eaten plain or "sandwiched"
with filling. Makes 2 dozen.

½ tsp cocoa
¼ tsp cinnamon
1½ cups unbleached flour
¾ 1½ cups unsalted butter
1 tsp grated lemon rind, orange rind, *or*
   grapefruit rind (I use whatever organically
   grown fruit is available)
½ tsp juice of whatever fruit you are using
¾ cup light brown sugar
½ cup walnuts, hazelnuts *or* almonds, ground
¼ cup homemade apricot jam *or* strawberry *or*
   raspberry jam (optional)
¾ lb semisweet chocolate (optional)
whole blanched almonds (optional)

Sift together the cocoa, cinnamon and flour; set aside.
   Preheat oven to 350°F. Cream the butter with
grated rind and fruit juice. Add sugar slowly and beat
until fluffy. Add ground nuts and dry ingredients; mix
well until blended. Let dough stand, covered, for 20
minutes. On a lightly floured baking board, roll dough
out to ¼″ thickness. Cut cookies with a 2½″ diameter
glass. Bake 15 minutes on a greased cookie sheet.
Transfer to rack and cool.
   To add filling: When cookies are cool, turn one
upside down and spread with ½ tsp jam, and cover
with a second cookie. For a really deluxe sandwich
cookie, melt semisweet chocolate and cover the sandwiched creation with it. Decorate each cookie with a
blanched almond.

Peanut Butter Cookies

Makes 1½ dozen.

½ cup unsalted butter *or* olive oil
1½ cups brown sugar
1 egg
½ cup peanut butter
1 cup unbleached flour
½ tsp sea salt
½ tsp baking soda

Preheat oven to 350°F. Mix butter and sugar. Add egg and beat well. Add peanut butter and blend. Add flour, salt and baking soda and work into dough. Form small balls, place on greased cookie sheet and press down with a fork. Bake 10–15 minutes.

Chocolate/Carob Chip Cookies

A favourite with the grandchildren, these cookies have the chocolate taste but, made with carob chips, also pass their mothers' inspection. Makes 4 dozen.

½ cup unsalted butter
½ cup brown sugar
1 tsp vanilla
1 egg
1¼ cups unbleached pastry flour
¼ tsp baking soda
½ tsp salt
½ cup carob chips *or* chocolate chips
½ cup chopped nuts (optional)

Preheat oven to 375°F. Cream butter, sugar and vanilla in medium bowl. Add egg and beat until light and fluffy. Blend dry ingredients into butter mixture; fold in carob chips and nuts. Drop batter from a teaspoon about 2" apart on lightly greased cookie sheet. Bake 8 minutes or until light golden brown.

Walnut Clusters

Delicious cookies! They are a great treat at Christmas. A box full of these cookies makes a special gift. Makes 2½ dozen.

½ cup sifted unbleached flour
¼ tsp baking powder
¼ tsp sea salt
¼ cup butter, softened
½ cup light brown sugar
1 egg
1½ tsp brandy
1½ squares unsweetened chocolate, melted
2 cups broken walnuts

Preheat oven to 350°F. Sift together flour, baking powder and salt. In a separate bowl, mix butter and sugar until creamy. Add egg and brandy. Mix in chocolate, then flour mixture. Fold in walnuts. Drop by teaspoonfuls, 1″ apart, onto greased cookie sheet. Bake just 10 minutes (no longer).

Jelly Drops

Here is another delicious cookie recipe, a great favourite with young and old. Makes 12–14 cookies.

½ cup light brown sugar
½ cup butter
1 egg
1 tsp vanilla *or* brandy
¾–1 cup unbleached flour
1 tsp baking powder
¾ cup arrowroot powder
pinch sea salt
jelly, jam *or* marmalade

Preheat oven to 350°F. Mix sugar and butter. Add egg, vanilla, flour, baking powder, arrowroot powder and salt. Drop in small balls on cookie sheet and press with thumb. Fill indentation with any kind of jelly, jam or marmalade. Bake on greased cookie sheet 10–12 minutes.

Nut and Raisin Cookies

Another very tasty treat! Makes 3 dozen.

1 cup butter, softened
2 cups light brown sugar
4 eggs
3¾ cups unbleached flour
1 tsp baking soda
1 tsp cinnamon
1 tsp nutmeg
½ tsp sea salt
¼ cup milk
1 cup chopped walnuts
2 cups dark raisins

In a large bowl, mix butter and sugar well. Add eggs and mix again. Add dry ingredients, *except* walnuts and raisins. Add milk, mixing well again. Add walnuts and raisins. Cover bowl and let stand in refrigerator overnight.

Preheat oven to 375°F. Drop by tablespoonfuls on greased cookie sheet, 1½" apart. Bake 15 minutes. Cool on a wire rack.

Walter's Cookies

My husband loves these cookies! I usually bake them for his hunting trips, as they are not only very nutritious, but also they keep well. However, as baked goods vanish very quickly at Copper Bay, spoilage has never been a concern! Makes 2 dozen.

1 cup butter
2 cups brown sugar
2 eggs
3¼ cups unbleached flour
1 tsp baking powder
½ tsp salt
1 cup chopped almonds

Cream butter and sugar, then add eggs. Add dry ingredients. Fold in almonds. Work well and shape into rolls. Let stand overnight in the refrigerator.

Preheat oven to 350°F. Slice rolls into cookies and bake on greased cookie sheet 20–25 minutes or until golden brown.

Shortbread

These are our grandson Séàn's cookies, rated as the very best! Makes 4 dozen.

2 cups unsalted butter, softened
1 cup light brown sugar
5 cups sifted unbleached flour (sift before
    measuring)

Beat the softened butter (a food processor on high speed works well) with the sugar until light and fluffy. Reduce speed to medium and add flour, ½ cup at a time. Beat until mixture is smooth. Roll the dough on a lightly floured board, about ½" thick.

Preheat oven to 350°F. Press or cut out your favourite shapes, place on greased cookie sheet and prick each piece several times with a fork. Bake 25–30 minutes in the middle of the oven. Cool completely on racks.

Almond Drops

Makes 6 dozen.

2 cups blanched almonds
½ cup glazed red cherries
1 cup unsalted butter
1 cup brown sugar, packed
½ tsp vanilla extract
½ tsp almond extract
2 eggs
2¼ cups sifted unbleached flour
½ tsp baking soda
¾ tsp sea salt

Chop almonds and cherries. Cream butter, sugar, vanilla and almond extract thoroughly. Add eggs one at a time, and continue creaming until light and fluffy. Sift together flour, baking soda and salt; add to the creamed mixture. Stir in nuts and cherries.

Preheat oven to 350°F. Drop dough by teaspoonfuls onto ungreased cookie sheets. Bake 12–15 minutes.

Carob Balls

These are Mary-Ann Coates's Christmas sweets, which were presented to me one year attractively arranged in a charming basket. A wonderful gift idea! Makes 2 dozen.

¼ cup butter
½ cup honey
1/3 cup carob powder
1⅓ cups non-instant milk powder
1¼ cups chopped nuts or seeds (I use walnuts)
2 tsp vanilla
½ cup unsweetened shredded coconut

Combine all ingredients except coconut. Mix well, then roll into balls and coat with coconut. Store them in the refrigerator.

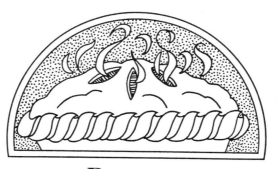

Desserts

Rhubarb Dessert

Our garden, even in the worst summers, always produces a wonderful and hardy crop of rhubarb. Here is our favourite dessert, unforgettable when served with whipped cream. Serves 6.

1 egg, well beaten
¾ cup + ⅓ cup brown sugar
½ cup + 2 tbsp unbleached flour
3 cups rhubarb, cut in ½" pieces
¼ cup butter

Preheat oven to 325°F. Combine the egg, ¾ cup of the brown sugar and 2 tbsp of the flour. Add rhubarb and place in a buttered casserole. Cream together the butter, the remaining ⅓ cup brown sugar, and the remaining ½ cup flour. Sprinkle this over the rhubarb mixture and bake 40 minutes, or until rhubarb is tender.

Orange Salad

Here is another elegant but "speedy" dessert. It is a great success whenever we serve it. We have found a place to buy the most delicious organically grown oranges, and I believe the quality of the fruit is the key to this dish. Serves 4–6.

    6 medium oranges
    4 tbsp brown sugar
    1 medium lemon
    4 tbsp coarsely chopped toasted almonds
    Grand Marnier (optional)

Peel 4 of the oranges. With a sharp knife, cut into thin slices across the segment. Remove the seeds and arrange slices in a shallow serving dish. Sprinkle with sugar. Finely grate the rind of half of the lemon and sprinkle over the oranges in the dish, along with the almonds. Squeeze the juice from the remaining two oranges and half the lemon, and pour over. Refrigerate until ready to serve. Turn the orange slices gently once or twice to mix with the liquid. For a special touch, add a little bit of Grand Marnier!

Apple Pudding

Our daughter Barbara adores this pudding. Regardless of the consequences, we indulge in it often. Serve it warm or cold, with or without whipping cream or homemade vanilla ice cream (see p. 152). Serves 4–6.

Pudding:
6 large apples, peeled and cored
cinnamon *or* nutmeg
¼ cup unsalted butter, softened
½ cup light brown sugar
1 egg, beaten
½ cup milk
1 cup unbleached pastry flour, sifted
2 tsp baking powder
¼ tsp sea salt
½ tsp vanilla extract

Sauce:
1 tbsp flour
1 cup brown sugar
1 tbsp butter
½ tsp vanilla
1½ cups water

To make the pudding, slice apples into a greased baking dish and sprinkle with cinnamon or nutmeg. Cream butter, sugar and egg together, then add milk alternately with sifted dry ingredients. Add vanilla. Spread over apples.

To make the sauce, combine all ingredients and boil for 5 minutes. Let cool and then pour over batter.

Preheat oven to 350°F. Bake 35–40 minutes.

Baked Apples in Maple Syrup

A delectable dessert, served warm or cold, fresh from the oven, or with whipped cream or ice cream (see p. 152). Serves 4.

    4 large golden delicious apples, washed and cored
      no deeper than ½" from the bottom
    2 tbsp grated lemon rind
    ¾ cup maple syrup

Preheat oven to 375°F.

Stand the apples in a buttered 8" x 8" baking dish. Spoon lemon rind over apples. Pour maple syrup into the cavities, and over the apples. Bake about 1 hour, basting every 10 minutes with the syrup.

Apple Charlotte

Serve this dessert, another of Mary Banks's pleasing recipes, with unsweetened whipped cream. Serves 4–6.

Butter a deep pie dish and fill with stewed, slightly sweetened apples. Cover with a layer of bread crumbs (the crust of white bread does nicely, otherwise use white crumbs). Add a sprinkling of soft brown sugar and apple pie spice, dot with butter and bake in a moderate oven until filling is hot. Then place the dish on the bottom shelf of the oven and heat the broiler to brown and crisp the Charlotte. The operative word is *brown*, not black, so watch *very* carefully.

Crumbly Crust Apple Pie

Also known as "Daddy's Favourite Dessert," this concoction is excellent served with ice cream (see p. 152), whipped cream, or just as it is. It is also delicious when fresh peaches are substituted for the apples. Serves 4–6.

6 cups sliced apples
1–2 tsp lemon juice
1 tsp cinnamon
¼ cup butter
½ cup unbleached flour
⅔ cup brown sugar

Preheat oven to 350 °F. Place sliced apples and lemon juice in a buttered 8″ casserole and sprinkle with cinnamon. Combine butter, flour and brown sugar and blend well to a crumbly mixture. Spread this on top of the apples and bake 45 minutes, or until apples are tender.

Apricot Squares

This delicious dessert is baked in two layers. I usually start the apricots for the topping before I make the base, so they have time to cool. These squares are perfect for a rainy weekend tea, when they are very much appreciated in front of a blazing fire. Serves 9.

Base:
½ cup unsalted butter
⅓ cup light brown sugar
1 cup unbleached flour, sifted
½ tsp vanilla

Topping:
⅔ cup chopped dried apricots
2 eggs, beaten
1 cup dark brown sugar, packed
⅓ cup unbleached flour, sifted
½ tsp baking powder
¼ tsp salt
½ cup chopped almonds
½ tsp vanilla

Preheat oven to 350°F. Lightly butter an 8″ x 8″ pan. To make the base, cream the butter with the sugar, then add flour and vanilla. Blend well and press into the pan. Bake 20 minutes.

To make the topping, cover apricots with water and boil 10–12 minutes. Drain and cool. Combine eggs with brown sugar and beat until light. Sift the flour, baking powder and salt together; add to the egg mixture. Fold in apricots, nuts and vanilla. Blend and spread evenly over the base. Return to the oven and bake 30–35 minutes. Cool and cut into squares.

Rice Pudding

Although we had an excellent cook at home and my mother's cooking was superlative, the most memorable meals of my childhood were the ones I ate at my maternal grandmother's house. Not only did Omi Kunzel run a beautiful home, she and her kitchen staff prepared the most delicious meals. I adored rice of any kind and in any form. The following dessert was prepared for me as often as I wished to have it. Serve it hot or cold with cream, fresh fruit, or any kind of homemade jam, or just as it is. My grandchildren adore it! Serves 4–6.

   1 cup brown rice
   2 cups water
   1 tsp sea salt
   1½ tsp brandy *or* cognac
   3 eggs
   ½ cup + 2 tbsp light brown sugar
   2 cups milk
   1 cup raisins
   1 tsp cinnamon
   butter

Cook the rice in the water and salt for 75 minutes. Drain and rinse at once in cold water.

Blend thoroughly the brandy, eggs and ½ cup of the sugar. Add milk and mix, then add cooked rice and raisins. Pour into prepared dish and top with the cinnamon and the remaining 2 tbsp sugar.

Preheat oven to 350°F. Dot the pudding with butter and bake 45 minutes.

Basic Pastry

When I started to cook for our guests at Copper Bay,
I had never baked a pie in my life. My mother was
a marvellous cook, but as a European she did not
know too much about pies. Nevertheless, she came
to my rescue by finding the following recipe. The
pastry has never let me down, whether I use it to
make a sweet pie or a quiche. Makes 2 pastry shells,
or one shell and one top crust.

2 cups unbleached flour, unsifted
⅓ tsp sea salt
½ cup shortening
⅓ cup butter
⅓ cup ice-cold water (approx.)

Sift flour and salt into a bowl. Cut in shortening and
butter with two knives or a pastry blender. When well
mixed, remove ½ cup of the mixture and set aside. To
the remainder, stir in ice-cold water, a little at a time,
until the dough forms a ball that cleans the bowl. With
as little handling as possible, form into a flat disc and
place on a lightly floured board. Roll out lightly in two
directions (away from you and toward you) to form a
large oval. Sprinkle evenly with the reserved dry
mixture and fold toward you.

Cut oval in half and seal the edges of each. Roll each
piece out to form a circle about ⅛" thick and 1–1½"
larger than a pie plate. Fit loosely into two pie plates,
pressing lightly but firmly into the bottom and sides.
Trim the edges and flute, or trim pastry so that it
extends past the edges by ½", then fold under and
crimp attractively. Prick bottom and sides in several
places if shells are to be baked before filling.

Blueberry Pie

Makes 1 pie (serves 6–8).

3 cups fresh blueberries *or* 2 boxes frozen,
   thawed blueberries
½ cup light brown sugar
2 tbsp unbleached flour
2 tbsp fresh lemon juice
1 tbsp butter, melted
¼ tsp sea salt
good dash of cinnamon
1 unbaked pastry shell with top crust

Preheat oven to 450°F. Combine all ingredients and fill pastry shell. Moisten edge of shell, cover with top crust and seal edges. Make several slits in the top crust and bake 20 minutes. Reduce oven temperature to 350°F and bake 20–25 minutes longer.

Mince Meat Pie

Agnes L. Mathers taught almost three generations in Sandspit, starting with a one-room school and finishing her career at the present Agnes L. Mathers School. She and her sister, Elizabeth (Jo) Kulik, became very dear friends of our family. It was a friendship that started when we became part of these enchanted islands, and ended with Jo's parting in 1981 and Agnes's death in 1984. The five of us (Agnes, Jo, Andrea, Barbara and myself) spent many happy hours in each other's kitchens cooking, laughing, reminiscing and listening to tales of long ago. Both sisters were excellent, resourceful cooks but their greatest quality was the love and consideration they put into their endeavours. The end product was always perfection – a work of art. This pie is one such recipe.

Mince Meat Pie has gained and lost the name "Mutton Pie" through the years. In the eighteenth century, it was baked under a long crust which was thought to represent the manger in Bethlehem, and its ingredients were symbols of the offerings made by the Magi. This recipe makes about 4 quarts.

1½ lbs almonds
1½ lbs dark sultanas
2 lbs raisins
5 lbs apples
2 tsp ground cloves
juice and grated rind of 2 oranges
juice and grated rind of 2 lemons
2 lbs beef suet
2 lbs brown sugar
½ cup molasses

2 tsp allspice
¾ tsp salt
½ cup brandy

Mix all ingredients together, *except* brandy, in a large bowl. Let stand overnight. In the morning, stir well, spoon into jars and pour brandy over the top of each for a seal. Cover and store in the refrigerator.

Pour into unbaked pastry shell and cover with top crust, using about 3 cups mince meat for a 9″ pie. Bake at 450°F for 10 minutes, then reduce heat to 350°F and bake 30 minutes longer.

Maple Cream Pie

An elegant, delicious and very Canadian dessert!
Makes 1 pie (serves 6–8).

Crust:
1¼ cups graham cracker crumbs
4 tbsp unsalted butter, melted
2 tbsp light brown sugar
¼ cup ground walnuts

Filling:
1 tbsp gelatin
¼ cup cold water
2 eggs, separated
pinch of salt
⅔ cup maple syrup
1 cup milk
½ cup whipping cream
1 tsp vanilla extract

Preheat oven to 300°F. Blend all crust ingredients well and press into bottom and sides of 9″ pie plate. Bake 15 minutes. Cool and chill for at least 1 hour.

To prepare the filling, soften gelatin in water. Beat egg yolks well, mix with the salt and ⅓ cup of the maple syrup, and pour into double boiler. Add milk gradually and blend well. Stir constantly over hot water until the mixture coats a spoon. Remove from heat, blend in gelatin. Chill 30 minutes.

Add the remaining ⅓ cup syrup and beat until smooth. Beat egg whites to stiff peaks and fold into the chilled maple mixture. Whip the cream with the vanilla, fold it into maple mixture and pour filling into prepared shell. Chill at least 3–4 hours.

Chocolate Loaf

Here is a truly elegant dessert. Dress it up even more by serving with whipped cream. Serves 8.

½ lb semisweet chocolate, cut into small pieces
¼ cup rum
1 cup unsalted butter, softened
2 tbsp superfine sugar
2 eggs, separated
1½ cups blanched almonds, pulverized in
    blender or with mortar and pestle
12 butter biscuits (Petits Beurre or Social Tea)
    cut into 1" x 1½" pieces
icing sugar
½ cup whipped cream (optional)

Lightly oil the bottom and sides of a 1½-quart loaf pan and invert the pan over paper towels to drain. In a heavy 1- to 1½-quart saucepan, melt the chocolate over low heat, stirring constantly. When all the chocolate is melted, stir in the rum and remove the pan from the heat. Cool to room temperature.

Cream the soft butter by beating it vigorously against the sides of a large mixing bowl until light and fluffy, or using a mixer. Beat in the sugar and then the egg yolks, one at a time. Stir in the almonds and cooled chocolate.

In a separate bowl, beat the egg whites with a rotary beater or wire whisk until they are stiff enough to cling to the beater in soft peaks. With a rubber spatula, fold them into the chocolate mixture. When no streaks of white show, gently fold in the cut-up biscuits. Spoon the mixture into the greased loaf pan and smooth the top with a spatula to spread it evenly. Cover tightly with plastic wrap and refrigerate for at least 4 hours, or until the loaf is firm.

Unmold the loaf 1 hour before serving time. Run a sharp knife around the sides of the pan and dip the bottom into hot water for a few seconds. Place a chilled serving platter upside down over the pan and, holding them together, quickly turn the plate and pan over. Rap the plate on the table; the loaf should slide out easily. If it does not, repeat the whole process. Smooth the top and sides of the unmolded loaf with a spatula, and return to the refrigerator. Before serving, sift a little icing sugar over the top.

Cut the loaf into thin slices before serving with whipped cream.

Isobel's Lemon Loaf

Serves 10.

6 tbsp shortening
1 cup sugar
2 eggs
sea salt to taste
½ cup milk
grated rind of 1 lemon
1½ tsp baking powder
1½ cups flour
¼ cup white sugar
juice of 1 lemon

Grease and flour a loaf pan. Combine shortening, sugar, eggs, salt, milk, lemon rind, baking powder and flour until well mixed. Place in loaf pan and let rise for 10 minutes.

Preheat oven to 400°F. Bake loaf 1 hour. Combine sugar and lemon, and while loaf is hot, brush lemon mixture over top.

Gugelhupf

Gugelhupf is a sugar-dusted cake with fluted wells and a hole in the middle. Traditionally it is made in several different sizes. It is as popular in Vienna today as it was during the reign of Emperor Franz Josef I, when the Emperor had a fresh one baked every day for his afternoon tea. Serves 10.

½ cup unsalted butter, softened
4 eggs, separated
½ cup light brown sugar
2 cups unbleached flour
1½ tsp baking powder
pinch of sea salt
½ cup milk
4 tbsp raisins
1 tsp vanilla
grated rind of 1 lemon
icing sugar (optional)

Preheat oven to 325°F. Beat butter, egg yolks and half the sugar until fluffy. In a separate bowl, beat egg whites until stiff. Fold gently into butter mixture. Combine the flour, baking powder and salt, and add to butter mixture alternately with the milk. Stir in raisins, vanilla and lemon rind. Pour batter into buttered and floured Gugelhupf form. Bake 1 hour or until tester comes out clean. Dust with icing sugar if desired.

Susie's Poppy Seed Cake

Serves 12.

Cake:
½ cup poppy seeds
1 cup milk
¾ cup margarine
1½ cups sugar
6 eggs, separated
2 cups flour
1 tsp salt
2 tsp baking powder

Filling:
½ cup sugar
1 tbsp cornstarch
1½ cups milk
1 tsp vanilla
½ cup walnuts

Preheat oven to 350°F. Soak seeds in milk. Beat margarine and sugar together; add 3 egg yolks. Sift together the flour, salt and baking powder. Add to the margarine mixture alternately with the seeds and milk mixture, ending with the dry ingredients. Beat egg whites until stiff; fold in. Bake 30–45 minutes or until done.

Combine the sugar and cornstarch. In a separate bowl, mix the milk and the 3 remaining egg yolks from the cake batter. Add the milk mixture slowly to the sugar mixture. In a saucepan, bring the mixture to a slow boil until thickened. Remove from heat and add vanilla and walnuts.

Cut cakes into halves, spread with filling and sandwich together.

Date-Nut Cake

A very delicious cake, suitable either for an after-noon tea or as a dessert. Serve it warm or cold. Serves 9.

Batter:
½ cup unsalted butter
½ cup light brown sugar
1 egg
1½ cups sifted unbleached flour
½ tsp sea salt
1½ tsp baking powder
½ cup milk

Filling:
½ cup brown sugar
1 tsp cinnamon
¼ cup chopped walnuts
1 tbsp flour
¼ cup butter, melted
¼ cup chopped dates

To make the batter, cream butter and sugar together. Beat well and add egg. Sift together flour, salt and baking powder. Add to sugar mixture, alternately with milk.

Preheat oven to 350°F. Combine all filling ingredients and mix well.

Spread half the batter in a greased 8″ square pan. Spread filling on top, then remaining batter. Bake 30 minutes.

Konigskuchen

Here is my mother's recipe for a loaf cake with almonds, raisins and rum. It makes one 10″ loaf.

butter, softened
¾ cup raisins
¾ cup currants
¼ cup dark rum *or* brandy *or* sherry
1 cup unsalted butter
1¼ cups light brown sugar
7 eggs, separated
1¾ cups unbleached flour
2½ tsp baking powder
¾ cup blanched almonds, pulverized in blender
    or with mortar and pestle
1 tsp grated lemon rind

Preheat oven to 325 °F. Generously butter the bottom and sides of a loaf pan with softened butter.

Combine raisins, currants and rum in a small bowl and soak 30 minutes. Cream the 1 cup unsalted butter and the sugar together in a large bowl until light and fluffy. Beat in the 7 egg yolks, one at a time, and continue beating for 10 minutes. Combine the flour and baking powder and beat into the sugar mixture, ¼ cup at a time. When the flour has been absorbed, stir in the raisins, currants, rum, almonds and lemon rind.

In a large bowl, beat the 7 egg whites until they form stiff peaks. Fold gently into the batter. Pour the batter into a loaf pan and bake in the middle of the oven for 1½ hours or until a tester comes out clean. Cool in the pan for 5 minutes. Run a sharp knife around the inside edges of the pan. Turn cake onto a rack to cool completely.

Carrot Cake

Everyone loves this wholesome cake, a special treat for nutrition enthusiasts. Serves 9.

1 cup grated carrot
1 cup light brown sugar *or* ¾ cup honey
¾ cup oil
2 eggs
juice and grated rind of 1 orange *or* 1 lemon
1½ cups unbleached flour
1 tsp baking soda
1 tsp baking powder
½ tsp salt
1 tsp cinnamon
½ cup chopped almonds
Egg-White Icing or Cream Cheese Topping
    (recipes follow)

Preheat oven to 350°F. Beat carrots, sugar, oil and eggs together and add juice and rind. Add dry ingredients and blend well. Pour into large loaf pan or 8″ square cake pan. Bake 50 minutes and cool. Top with your favourite icing.

Egg-White Icing

Delicious, and sans icing sugar!

1 egg white
⅛ tsp sea salt
½ cup liquid honey, warmed
¼ tsp vanilla extract

Beat egg white with salt until peaks form. Add honey in a thin, constant stream while continuing to beat. Add vanilla and continue beating until thick.

Cream Cheese Topping

Beat 8 oz cream cheese until fluffy. Gradually beat in 2–3 tbsp maple syrup.

Copper Bay Cheesecake

This is a rich dessert, best served after a light main course. Serves 9.

22 graham wafers, crushed (1½–1¾ cups)
3 tbsp unsalted butter, melted
16 oz cream cheese
1 scant cup light brown sugar
2 eggs, separated
1 cup light cream
1 tsp vanilla extract *or* cognac

Mix wafer crumbs and butter. Pat into the bottom of a greased 8″ square cake pan. Reserve enough crumbs for sprinkling on top. Cream the cheese well and beat in sugar, egg yolks, cream and vanilla. Beat egg whites until they stand in peaks. Fold into the cheese mixture.

Preheat oven to 350°F. Spoon cheese mixture into crust and smooth it. Sprinkle reserved crumbs on top. Bake 25–30 minutes or until set.

My Mother's Apple Cheesecake

*This is another recipe from my childhood. Tradition-
ally, the cake was served on Saturday afternoons for
kaffee, usually during the winter months when no fresh
fruit was available to make fruit-torten. Serves 9.*

Base:
1½ cups unbleached flour
⅓ cup unsalted butter
½ cup light brown sugar
pinch of sea salt
1 tbsp dark rum
1 egg
6 apples, peeled and cut into wedges

Topping:
24 oz cream cheese, softened
2 cups milk
1 cup sour cream
1¼–1½ cups light brown sugar
3 eggs, separated
vanilla pudding, made from 1 pkg non-instant pudding
1 tsp baking powder

To make the base, mix flour, butter, sugar, salt, rum and
egg well and refrigerate for ½–1 hour. On a lightly
floured surface, roll the dough into a disc, and press into
a buttered springform pan. Layer apples on top of dough.

Preheat oven to 325°F. To make the topping, mix
cream cheese, milk, sour cream and sugar. Add egg yolks
and the prepared pudding. Sprinkle baking powder over
all and mix well. In a separate bowl, beat egg whites until
they form stiff peaks. Fold gently into batter. Pour over
apples, bake 75–90 minutes and let cool in oven.

Linzertorte

One Christmas when our children were very young, we received a wonderful gift box from Walter's mother and an elderly aunt. Omi Pottendorf, as my mother-in-law was affectionately called by our girls, and Tante Mitze had produced a Viennese Christmas bake shop. Looking at the quantity, we thought it must have taken them weeks to prepare all those delectable goodies. One of the treasures in the parcel was a Linzertorte. Whenever I see or taste that particular cake, my memories take me back to that Christmas of long ago, and to the two dear people who made it so special. The cake keeps for several weeks and travels well! Serves 9.

    2 cups unbleached flour
    ¾ cup unsalted butter, cold
    ¾ cup light brown sugar
    ¾ cup almonds, pulverized in blender or with
        mortar and pestle
    grated rind of ½ lemon
    grated rind of ½ orange
    2 eggs
    1 tsp cinnamon
    ¼ tsp allspice
    ¼ tsp cloves
    1 cup thick raspberry *or* red currant jam
        (homemade is best)
    icing sugar

Line a 10″ springform pan with buttered waxed paper. Sift flour into a mixing bowl. Cut butter into small pieces and add to flour. Stir in sugar. Knead with your hands until the dough is smooth and forms a ball. Add almonds, grated rinds, eggs and spices. Continue to beat until mixture is smooth and doughy. Form into a ball, wrap in waxed paper and refrigerate 1–2 hours to firm dough.

Preheat oven to 350°F. Press three-quarters of the dough into the lined pan. Divide the remainder of the dough into 6 equal parts. Use 2 parts to make a ¾″ high edge for the torte, pressing it into the sides of the pan. Cover the surface of the dough on the bottom with jam. Use the other four pieces of dough to create a lattice effect on top of the jam layer.

Bake 45 minutes. Test the edge for doneness before removing the cake from the oven. Loosen the spring-form edge of the pan and, while the torte is still hot, sprinkle with icing sugar.

Ice Cream

This ice cream is an old recipe from my mother. It was the highlight of a weekend to get a serving or two at tea-time on a Sunday afternoon. You may substitute any kind of fruit for the glazed mixed fruit. When you use berries, omit the vanilla, almonds and almond extract. Sprinkle berries with 1 tbsp cognac. Serves 8–10.

1½ cups finely chopped glazed mixed fruits
2 tsp vanilla extract
1 tsp almond extract
3 cups chilled whipping cream
½ cup light brown sugar
½ cup blanched, roasted almonds, pulverized in
   the blender or with a mortar and pestle

In a small mixing bowl, sprinkle the glazed fruits with the vanilla and almond extracts and let them soak at least 20 minutes. In a large, chilled mixing bowl, beat the whipping cream until it begins to thicken. Gradually beat in the sugar, a tablespoon at a time, and continue to beat until the cream holds fairly firm peaks when the beater is lifted out of the bowl. With a rubber spatula, fold in the glazed fruit mixture and the ground almonds until the ingredients are well combined. Spoon the mixture into a 1½-quart soufflé dish, smooth the top, and cover with plastic wrap or foil. Freeze for at least 5 hours. The concoction must be firm.

Run a spatula around the inside edge of the ice cream to unmold. Then dip the bottom of the mold into hot water for 15 seconds. Wipe the mold dry and invert a flat serving plate on top of it. Grasping mold and plate firmly together, turn them over. The ice cream should slide out easily. Cut into pie-shaped wedges with a knife that has been dipped in hot water.

Health Candy

Makes 24 candies.

¼ cup unsalted butter
1 cup liquid honey
1 cup ground flax seed (available at health food stores)
1 cup wheat germ
1 cup unsweetened shredded coconut *or* ground almonds

Melt butter and brown slightly; remove from heat and stir in honey until melted. Combine flax seed and wheat germ and add to honey mixture. Stir and shape into small balls. Roll in coconut or ground almonds. Keep covered in the refrigerator.

Egg Kognak

When I was growing up, it was a family Christmas tradition to serve this festive concoction to our visitors. Serves 12.

4 egg yolks
1 tsp vanilla
1 tbsp + 1½ cups light brown sugar
2 cups milk
1½ cups brandy *or* cognac

Beat egg yolks with vanilla and 1 tbsp of the sugar. In a saucepan, bring milk and remaining sugar to the boiling point, stirring constantly. Add to egg mixture very slowly. Beat until cool; add brandy. Stir until blended. Store in bottles in a cool place.

Didi's Biscuits

For our four-legged friends, companions and guests, we try to keep some of these goodies on hand. Didi, our springer spaniel, adores them. Makes 36 biscuits.

2 cups whole wheat flour
¼ cup wheat germ
½ cup soy flour
1 tsp brewer's yeast
1 tsp sea salt
¼ cup rolled oats
2 tbsp oil
¼ cup molasses
½ cup chopped dried fruit (Didi's favourite is apricots)
2 eggs
¼ cup milk

Mix dry ingredients together, then add oil, molasses and dried fruit. In a separate bowl, combine eggs and milk. Reserve 1 tbsp of this mixture, and add the remainder to the dough. Knead for a few minutes and let the dough rest for at least 30 minutes.

Preheat oven to 350°F. Roll out dough ½" thick and cut into shapes. Brush with the reserved egg-milk mixture and bake 30 minutes or until lightly browned. To make harder biscuits, turn off the heat and leave them in the oven for 1 hour or longer.

Index